The Uses of Instructional Objectives

A PERSONAL PERSPECTIVE

W. JAMES POPHAM
Professor of Education
University of California, Los Angeles

FEARON PUBLISHERS

Lear Siegler, Inc., Education Division • Belmont, California

Copyright © 1973, by Fearon Publishers/Lear Siegler, Inc.,
Education Division, 6 Davis Drive, Belmont, California 94002.
All rights reserved. No part of this book may be reproduced
by any means, nor transmitted, nor translated into a machine
language, without written permission from Fearon Publishers.

ISBN-0-9224-1685-9

Library of Congress Catalog Card Number: 72-95013.

Printed in the United States of America.

Contents

Preface

In 1959 I was a faculty member at Kansas State College of Pittsburg, my first teaching position after the completion of graduate school. At that time sporadic reports were beginning to come in about a new instructional development that was attracting much public and professional attention—teaching machines. I tried to find out more about these devices, but such information was hard to come by then, particularly in Pittsburg, Kansas. I was able to locate some of the early articles on teaching machines, thereby discovering that the machine was merely a program holder and that the heart of this new approach was its effort to apply laboratory principles of behavior modification to the classroom instruction of children. Programmed instruction, not teaching machines, was the real innovation and I was fascinated by its possibilities.

The truly intriguing feature of programmed instruction, at least to me, was that it provided a strategy for devising instructional sequences which could, sooner or later, be improved to the point where they were *demonstrably* effective. Having taught previously in both high school and college, where I carried on my teaching responsibilities largely on an intuitive basis, the prospect of discovering a more systematic approach to instruction was magnetic.

In brief, programmed instruction first called for the assertion of one's instructional intentions in explicit language—in other words, it required the instructor to state an objective in terms of measurable learner behavior. Then the programmer devised a replicable instructional sequence —that is, one not heavily dependent on a teacher's personal expertise. This sequence was then tried out with learners and revised (on the basis of whether the specified objective was achieved) until it eventually accomplished its objective. Programmed instruction was, therefore, a highly empirical method of designing instruction, for it provided an explicit criterion (the pre-set instructional objective) against which the adequacy of one's instructional efforts could be evaluated. Enthralled with the probable potency of this new approach, I read everything I could get my hands on that pertained to programmed instruction.

Upon moving to San Francisco State College in 1960, I soon discovered that there was much more interest in programmed instruction on the West Coast than there had been in Kansas. Conversely, of course, there was far less interest in growing corn. I soon met a dapper fellow named Robert Mager, who was working as a training psychologist. Bob asked me if he could try out an early version of a little book that he was writing which dealt with instructional objectives. It was in a programmed format and he was anxious to get some evidence as to how effective it was. I was then teaching an introductory course dealing with programmed instruction (the newness of the field having permitted me to move from my position of abject ignorance of the subject in 1959 to instant expertise in 1960), and the course was ideal for Bob's field test.

I still recall his observations that day as we watched my students wade through a mimeographed version of what was to become, in my estimate, the single most influential book in acquainting educators with the nature of measurable objectives. Bob opined that when all the fuss over teaching machines and programmed instruction had died down, the major contribution of the movement would be its emphasis on measurable instructional objectives. I believe that events of the 1960's have supported his prophecy.

For my own professional life, those were influential days. Although measurable instructional objectives could not provide all the answers to America's educational shortcomings, I saw them as a powerful tool which could yield curricular, instructional, and evaluation dividends for educators. In the early 1960's I spent a fair amount of time clarifying my own thinking regarding the ways that explicit instructional objectives could be profitably employed. There were a number of courses, workshops, speeches, and other activities in which I tried to expose people to the potential raptures of measurable instructional goals.

I found that the use of measurable objectives markedly influenced my own teaching, and when I moved to UCLA in 1962 I organized all my instructional efforts around measurably formulated objectives. This resulted in the design of courses which, in time, became more effective in promoting learner attainment of those objectives. My practice of always disclosing course objectives to my students led to a less anxious and generally more positive student clientele. By this time I was personally hooked on the merits of explicit instructional objectives.

By the mid-sixties I tried to endorse such objectives more deliberately through the development of programmed filmstrip-tape programs which focused on how to formulate objectives and by writing essays on the applications of such goal statements. Most of those essays have been gathered together in the following pages. They deal with such topics as the background of the measurable objectives movement, curricular and instructional uses of objectives, the role of objectives in educational management, the concomitants of precise objectives in measurement and evaluation, objectives selection versus objectives generation, and objectives-based approaches to teacher appraisal.

Since these essays span a number of years, the attentive reader will note some position-shifting going on. Hopefully, these modifications in stance reflect the natural changes that would be anticipated when one's ideas are tested over the years. And tested these ideas have been. I once thought that by the close of the 1960's the educational community would have tired of the topic of instructional goals. This does not appear to be the case. In traveling around the country I find, if anything, an intensified interest in the potential contributions of measurable instructional objectives, their strengths and their weaknesses.

It is in that context that I agreed to put together my chief writings on the topic of instructional objectives. As the title of this book suggests, it represents a highly personal set of perspectives on the educational roles of instructional objectives. That there will be disagreements with the views represented in the following pages is certain. I only hope that these perspectives will stimulate the kind of dialogue regarding instructional goals that will eventually result in improved education. For that, you see, is my objective.

w.j.p.

PART ONE

Instructional Objectives
in Perspective

The three articles in this section set the stage for the remainder of the book by looking back at education's behavioral objectives movement of the 1960's. The initial essay, "Instructional Objectives, 1960–1970," examines a decade of concern and controversy regarding objectives, while the second, "Objectives '72," tries to bring the reader up to date regarding recent developments. The third selection deals with the specific question of whether all objectives must be stated in measurable form, and attempts to trace the writer's thoughts regarding this issue.

1

Instructional Objectives, 1960-1970

Without question the most important instructional advance in America during the 1960's was a widespread advocacy and increased use of measurable instructional objectives. There will be those, of course, who point out that support for measurable objectives was not an event peculiar to the past decade. Indeed, educational historians have located the pronouncements of many of our educational predecessors who have argued for explicitly stated instructional goals. The possibility always exists that an archeologist will someday unearth a prehistoric potsherd with an inscription supporting high-level cognitive outcomes. On the other hand, almost any phenomenon can be dismissed by the "it's nothing new" detractors. What marked the 1960's as unique with respect to instructional objectives was a coalescing of educational support; that is, the emergence of a critical mass of advocates who fostered clearly explicated goals. And in promoting the use of measurable instructional objectives, the programmed instruction movement should receive principal credit.

In spite of certain educators' advocacy of behavioral objectives during earlier eras, it took the enthusiasm of the programmed instruction devotees to really get many people talking about measurable goals. In fact, nothing illustrates this quite so well as Robert Mager's volume which was originally entitled *Preparing Objectives for Programmed Instruction* and which later became *Preparing Instructional Objectives*. The text was devised initially for programmers but subsequently won acceptance from many educators involved in non-programmed instruction. Rarely during the history of education has a book with fewer pages and more white space been as influential on the thinking and practice of American educators. Mager's sixty-two page opus not only contained a very readable message, but it provided the reader with several practical skills—skills

Reprinted from the July, 1970, issue of *National Society for Programmed Instruction Journal*, Vol. IX, No. 6, p. 5.

which most teachers did not possess. In a field where demonstrable competencies are the exception rather than the rule, it is small wonder that so many educators responded positively to this book.

Bloom's *Cognitive Taxonomy of Educational Objectives* had been available since 1956, but until programmed instruction enthusiasts began to press for specificity, interest in the cognitive taxonomy was minimal. The publication of Krathwohl's *Affective Taxonomy of Educational Objectives* in 1964 was important in that it reemphasized the necessity for attending to diverse kinds of instructional goals and, in general, added to the general interest in objectives. But programmed instruction proponents were the most vocal supporters of explicitly stated goals. Without their efforts both taxonomies might have languished in educational oblivion.

Many educators who found themselves drawn to the value of explicit instructional objectives, both for originally planning an instructional sequence and for subsequently evaluating whether that sequence was effective, were stunned in the mid-sixties to discover that there were alien forces present. There were people who were actually counseling *against* the use of behavioral objectives! Among the criticisms of measurable objectives was the contention that rigid prespecifications for instruction would tend to reduce the flexibility of our educational offerings. More significant, perhaps, was the criticism that an emphasis on behavioral objectives would draw educators toward pedestrian, more easily operationalized objectives rather than high-level, difficult-to-measure goals. One must report, in fairness, that despite the tremendous beneficial influences Bob Mager's book has had, there have been some deleterious side effects. The vast majority of Mager's examples tend to deal with rather low-level instructional outcomes. There were some readers who erroneously assumed that a proponent of measurable instructional objectives had to, of necessity, endorse the most prosaic kinds of goals.

Thus, a rather vigorous debate emerged. Proponents defended measurable objectives on the grounds that they were a *sine qua non* in any rational plan of instruction and evaluation. In contrast, there was a smaller but vocal group (Eisner, 1966) who contended that a heavy emphasis upon measurable instructional objectives would, ultimately, prove detrimental to the progress of education.

Although heated, the controversy proved relatively unproductive. Most individuals working with measurable objectives today realize that there are some educational goals that are so worthwhile that they ought to be pursued even though our current measurement sophistication does not permit a rigorous assessment. A reasonable proportion of any class instruction might legitimately be directed toward the promotion of such currently unassessable goals. On the other hand, proponents of behavioral objectives wish to reduce the enormous proportion of classroom instruction currently directed toward unmeasurable goals.

Essentially, then, the early sixties were marked by the initial proselyting efforts of behavioral objectives advocates, particularly those associated with the programmed instruction movement. The mid-sixties saw the development of a controversy regarding the merits of measurable objectives, a controversy that has lingered to some extent.

But the most important obvious phenomenon of the mid-1960's was an increasing acceptance of measurable educational objectives by influential American educators. There were myriad workshops and short courses on instructional objectives, usuallly offered for public school teachers and administrators. An increasing number of instructional materials began to appear which explained the essentials of measurable goals and thus permitted large numbers of individuals to become conversant with the technical requisites of a well formulated objective. The U.S. Office of Education became enamoured of measurable instructional objectives, urging project officials in a number of their enterprises to specify their goals in measurable terms. Educators throughout the land began to view behavioral objectives not as unknowns or fads, but as potentially useful instructional assets.

Yet, close observation of the educational scene permitted a disquieting inference. Though many educators were now familiar with the procedures involved in specifying measurable objectives, relatively few instructors were actually using them. For some of us, this observation proved more than casually disturbing. We had informed, urged, cajoled, and lauded the use of measurable objectives, but there were relatively few takers. Painful reappraisal of the instructional scene yielded a possible interpretation. We were asking more than could be reasonably granted by practicing educators. We were asking teachers and administrators to take on a new and very difficult job in addition to their current responsibilities. Anyone who has seriously engaged in the preparation of measurable instructional objectives knows how difficult it is. We were asking already harassed educators to take on this onerous task. The request was unreasonable.

Consequently, about three years ago, several of us started recommending that whereas it might be unrealistic to expect teachers to be *generators* of their own objectives, it was possible that they could become *selectors* of such measurable goals. Accordingly, the Instructional Objectives Exchange was formed as a depository of instructional objectives which would permit educators to examine a wide range of measurable instructional goals and to select those behavioral objectives suitable for their own instructional purposes.

Originally established by the UCLA Center for the Study of Evaluation, the Instructional Objectives Exchange is now a nonprofit educational corporation and currently has sixteen collections of measurable objectives. Each objective is accompanied by a sample test item and, in some cases, five or more additional items for assessing each objective's attainment.

As a result of the increasing acceptance of measurable instructional objectives, it is not surprising that we would be obliged to learn more about them. As a consequence of our increased knowledge regarding the formulation and assessment of such objectives we have encountered certain problems. Several of these difficulties will now be examined.

Minimal Proficiency Levels

Bob Mager indicated in his slender antidote to confusion that one of the required elements of a well-stated objective was that minimum level of proficiency should be identified. This is easier to recommend than to accomplish. One can recall the military's early emphasis upon a 90-90 proficiency level wherein 90 percent of the learners had to score 90 percent or better on the criterion test prior to the use of certain programmed instruction materials. Whereas there is a degree of implied rigor in a 90-90 proficiency level, any careful analysis of that scheme for setting proficiency levels will reveal that the standard is totally dependent upon the difficulty of the examination and, as such, is more deceptive than clarifying. There are a host of situations in which 90 percent of the learners do not need to attain 90 percent proficiency. On the other hand, there are instances in which 100 percent of the learners must perform with perfection.

There are some situations in which an external criterion, such as post-instruction job requirements, determine how well students should perform. There are other instances in which the nature of subsequent instructional sequences dictate the level of proficiency required. But for the vast majority of instructional situations, we have few rules to guide us in how to describe expected levels of competency.

One distinction that has proved serviceable to some is the contrast between *student* and *class minimal levels*. We can identify the level of proficiency required by an individual learner in order for him to reflect satisfactory attainment of a goal, but it is usually also necessary to indicate the level of proficiency expected for an entire group of learners in order that an instructional sequence can be considered acceptable.

Clearly, there are many instances in which not every learner will achieve the desired level of proficiency. We would obviously not revise our instructional procedures any time fewer than 100 percent of the learners displayed the desired skill on an objective. More attention in the 1970's should be given to refining technical procedures for identifying both student and class proficiency levels.

Content Generality

One of the difficulties with our early techniques for stating objectives is that we tended to make an objective essentially equivalent to a test item, for example, "A student will be able to list the names of five former NSPI presidents." The fact that such an objective, albeit measurable, was nothing more than a test item did not disturb us in the early sixties. Perhaps this was because we were trying to describe how objectives should be stated rather than putting them into practice on a wide-scale basis. Now we find educational systems in which there is a real desire to organize instruction around such goals and the practical problem of how many such objectives can be managed presents itself.

Eva Baker (1968) has argued that to be maximally serviceable, objectives should possess not *test item equivalence* but *content generality*. An objective possessing content generality describes a range of specific kinds of learner responses rather than a single test item. There are unresolved questions regarding what level of generality should be employed so that objectives are both useful in promoting clarity of intent and also parsimoniously usable by educators. Our attention should be directed toward these issues.

Measuring the Attainment of Objectives

One of the very desirable features of the programmed instruction movement is that it has promoted revised conceptions of measurement. These notions of measurement are predicated upon the clearly stated objectives which are so prevalently employed in programmed instruction. Indeed, Robert Glaser's (1963) article in the *American Psychologist* stimulated considerable interest in the kind of measurement that was suitable for assessing the quality of instructional enterprises rather than discriminating among individuals. This contrast between norm-reference measurement and criterion-referenced measurement (Popham and Husek, 1969) has demonstrated dramatically how our current measurement technology is designed for a system of test construction and test improvement which has purposes other than measuring the quality of instructional programs. Mechanisms such as item-analysis procedures and internal-consistency estimates, as well as the standard notions of validity and reliability, are not pertinent to the kinds of measurement procedures that must be used to assess the attainment of measurable instructional objectives. A great deal of sophisticated work needs to be done regarding how to devise classes of measures that satisfactorily serve to sample the behavior and content domains delimited by a well-stated objective.

In attempting to deal with this crucial question, most progress has been made by Wells Hively and his associates (1970) at the University of Minnesota. But more resources need to be devoted to such questions. It is far too easy to employ measurable instructional objectives as a facade for "instruction as usual." We must discover efficient ways to produce satisfactory measures of such objectives so that they can be economically assessed.

It has been observed elsewhere that one of the consoling features of conventional instruction is that it is typically so impotent one need not worry too much about what it is attemping to accomplish. Our instructional technology has been sharpened during the past decade and our objectives have become more clear. An unexpected but important dividend has been yielded by the continuing emphasis upon measurable objectives. We are discovering improved ways of identifying what objectives *ought* to be taught. The clarity that has accompanied measurable objectives has permitted the evaluation of such objectives in a number of heretofore untried ways. Technical schemes (Popham, 1969) for initially identifying the instructional goals that are most defensible have been devised and are apparently proving usable. For example, we can now secure very precise ratings of the curricular worth of sets of measurable objectives from diverse groups, such as, learners, teachers, community leaders, and so on. Such ratings can be contrasted with actual assessments of learners' pre-instruction abilities to master each objective. Given such preference and performance data, far more enlightened curricular decisions can result.

One of the often heard phrases of the past few years has been *educational accountability*. Educational accountability in this instance means that the instructional system designers take responsibility for achieving the kinds of instructional objectives that are previously explicated. Indeed, the whole notion of educational accountability is inextricably wedded to measurable goals. The interest of state legislatures in such accountability will undoubtedly yield even more attention to measurable objectives in the future. For example, the state of Florida now requires specific instructional objectives in order for public school courses to be accredited. Similarly, the state of California has undertaken an extensive investigation regarding the manner in which its educational goals can first be identified in measurable terms and then subsequently measured. This approach toward accountability is quite gratifying, but will make necessary, even more dramatically, the solution of current and emerging technical questions associated with precise educational objectives.

Whereas in the 1960's we witnessed the birth and early development of the instructional objectives movement, it appears that the 1970's will represent this movement's post-pubescent period. There will be less drum pounding and more systematic progress toward a really usable technology of instructional objectives. The educational consumer has demonstrated a clear interest in objectives; now we have to refine the product so that it is attractive and nourishing—and leaves no unpleasant aftertaste.

References

BAKER, EVA, "Defining Content for Objectives" (Los Angeles: Vimcet Associates, P.O. Box 24714, 1968).

BLOOM, BENJAMIN S. *et al., Taxonomy of Educational Objectives, Handbook I: Cognitive Domain* (New York: David McKay, 1956).

EISNER, E.W., "Educational Objectives: Help or Hinderance?" (Paper read at the annual meeting of the American Educational Research Association, Chicago, February, 1966).

GLASER, ROBERT, "Instructional Technology and the Measurement of Learning Outcomes: Some Questions." *American Psychologist* 18, 1963, pp. 519–21.

HIVELY, WELLS II, "Domain-Referenced Achievement Testing" (A symposium chaired by Wells Hively II at the annual meeting of the American Educational Research Associates, Minneapolis, March, 1970).

KRATHWOHL, DAVID R., *et al., Taxonomy of Educational Objectives, Handbook II: Affective Domain* (New York: David McKay, 1964).

MAGER, ROBERT F., *Preparing Instructional Objectives* (Belmont, Calif.: Fearon Publishers, 1962).

POPHAM, W. JAMES, "Educational Needs Assessment in the Cognitive, Affective, and Psychomotor Domains" (A presentation at three ESEA Title III Regional Workshops sponsored by the U.S. Office of Education, 1969).

POPHAM, W. JAMES, and T.R. HUSEK, "Implications of Criterion-Referenced Measurement." *Journal of Educational Measurement* 6 (Spring 1969) pp. 1–9.

2

Objectives '72

When Sergio Mendes and his highly successful musical group Brasil '66 decided to change their name to Brasil '77, they admitted that their prime motive was to maintain an up-to-date image. Mendes and his promoters recognized that potential record purchasers of the seventies might view recordings from a sixties group as more worthy of historical veneration than purchase.

In the field of education there is a comparable danger that when one considers the topic of instructional objectives images may arise that were more appropriate for the 1960's than for today. Instructional objectives '72 are not instructional objectives '62. And the educator who, basing his decision on an outdated notion of objectives, judges the relevance of instructional objectives to his current concerns will likely make the wrong decision. In the following paragraphs an effort will be made to inspect some of the more recent wrinkles in the rapidly changing countenance of instructional objectives. By considering a potpourri of contemporary conceptions and uses of instructional objectives, today's educator will, we hope, remain *au courant*.

In the early and mid-sixties there was a goodly amount of excitement about instructional objectives, particularly *behavioral* objectives. America's educators had located a new tool for their instruction kit—that is, objectives stated in terms of learner post-instruction behavior—and many teachers were truly enthralled by the new toy. During that period there were enough "how-to-write-'em" workshops to stuff a horse. With few exceptions, horse stuffing might have been a more beneficial pursuit. This was the era of drum pounding, and (speaking as a former drum pounder) many zealots viewed behavioral objectives as the first step on a stairway to educational paradise.

Reprinted from the March, 1972, issue of *Phi Delta Kappan*. Copyright 1972 by Phi Delta Kappa, Inc.

We'll never know whether the remarkable display of interest in behavioral objectives was caused by (1) the activities of programmed instructional enthusiasts (who universally employed behavioral objectives), (2) the impact of Robert Mager's little self-instruction book[1] on how to state objectives (which could be completed in 45 minutes, hence was praiseworthy on brevity grounds alone), (3) the markedly increased sales of the *Taxonomies of Educational Objectives*[2] (which may have made professors Bloom, Krathwohl, *et al.* regret their nonroyalty contracts with the publishers), or (4) the insistence of many U.S. Office of Education officials that instructional project proposals had to include behavioral objectives (which proposal writers often did, but project staffs often forgot).

Whatever the causes, many of our nation's educators became behavioral-objectives enthusiasts. Everywhere one turned, a speaker was expounding the raptures of behavioral goals. The professional literature abounded with articles on objectives. A flood of books and filmstrips told how to state objectives behaviorally. "Behavioral" and "objectives" were, without challenge, the most persistent educational buzz words of the mid-sixties.

But much of the agitation about instructional objectives has abated. No longer behaving like newlyweds, educators and objectives are learning how to live with each other an a more permanent post-honeymoon basis. It will be interesting to see whether in this instance familiarity breeds contempt or contentment.

Most knowledgeable proponents of explicit instructional objectives have veered away from using the phrase *behavioral objectives,* for they recognize that some educators erroneously equate the adjective "behavioral" with a mechanistic, dehumanized form of behaviorism. What most objectives enthusiasts want is only *clarity regarding instructional intentions,* not a stipulation of the strategy (such as behaviorism) used to accomplish those intentions. Thus, because such phrases create less misdirected resistance, expressions similar to "performance objectives," "measurable objectives," or "operational objectives" are often employed these days.

Some educators use the terms *objectives, goals, aims, intents,* and so on, interchangeably. Others use the terms differently, depending on the level of generality involved. For instance, *goal* is used by some to convey a broader instructional intention, while *objective* is reserved for more limited classroom instruction. Anyone involved in a discussion of these topics had best seek early clarification of the way the terms are being employed.

But irrespective of the particular phrase employed to depict precise instructional objectives, there are still a number of people who, individually or collectively, find fault with such goals. Some critics deal with particular technical issues such as the nature of the logical connections between the goal that is sought and the pupil behaviors that are used to indicate whether the goal has been realized. In a similar vein, other writers raise questions regarding the optimal level of generality at which objectives should be explicated—that is, how can objectives be both precise enough to communicate unambiguously and broad enough to avoid the thousands of objectives that would surely follow if each objective equaled a single test item. These forms of criticism are useful to those educators who would work with measurable instructional objectives, for the problems identified must be solved, at least partially, to increase the educational utility of objectives. And even in the enlightened seventies it must be noted that there are a number of technical problems regarding the uses of instructional objectives that have not yet been satisfactorily resolved, the generality-level dilemma being a good illustration.

But there are other types of critics. Anointing themselves as Defenders of the Faith, these people view proponents of performance objectives as minions of an unseen force commissioned to destroy our currently laudable educational enterprises.[3] These critics engage in all the classic forms of nonrational debate, either deliberately erecting straw men or displaying remarkable misinformation regarding current thinking on the topic of instructional objectives.

Certainly, there are abuses of instructional objectives. These are usually perpetrated by administrators who, having read Mager's little volume on objectives, feel themselves blessed with instant expertise and thus institute a freewheeling objectives circus in their schools. Surely, there are too many examples of trivial behavioral objectives which, albeit measurable, no clear-thinking educator should ever pursue. Clearly, there are too few illustrations of really high-level cognitive goals or important affective goals. But these are rectifiable deficiencies. Those critics who wish to chuck the whole notion of measurable objectives because of such deficits would probably have rejected forever all antibiotics because some early versions of these medications were less than perfect.

One hopes that groups such as the National Council of Teachers of English, who at their national convention in 1970 passed a resolution rejecting behavioral objectives almost *in toto*, will reappraise their stance. While teachers in fields such as English do find it difficult to frame some of their more important intentions in a form which permits subsequent assessment, they should not be excused from the task. Nor should they be applauded when they cast behavioral objectives proponents in the

Arthurian role of the wicked knight. It is devilishly hard to assess many of the more profound goals of education. But if we can make some progress toward doing so, then we shall surely reap dividends for education and the learners it should serve.

Objectives Depositories

One development that seems to be catching on in educational circles is the establishment of objectives bank agencies or test item depositories.[4] These organizations collect large numbers of objectives and measuring instruments, thereafter making them available so that educators may select those materials of particular use in a local educational setting. The heavy demand for materials distributed by such agencies as the Instructional Objectives Exchange suggests that American educators are finding these sorts of support materials useful.

There are some critics of precise objectives who find the provision of "ready-made" objectives particularly reprehensible. These individuals contend that it is demeaning for teachers to select their objectives from an extant pool of goals. Teachers, they argue, should personally devise their own statements of objectives. This form of carping, it strikes me, is akin to asking a surgeon to manufacture his own surgical instruments. If I am about to undergo an appendectomy, I would prefer that the scalpel to be used had been professionally prepared by a surgical instrument manufacturer instead of pounded out in my doctor's toolshed. For that is precisely what objectives depositories are attempting to provide—*tools* for instructional designers and evaluators. The statements of objectives and pools of test items can be used, modified, or rejected by educators, depending on the suitability of the tools for a given instructional situation. To reject the provision of such tools is to yearn for the pre-hand-axe society of primitive man.

Accountability Equals Objectives?

For some educators, the notion of explicit instructional objectives is inextricably tied up with the recent concern about educational accountability. They hear accountability enthusiasts attempting to devise educational monitoring systems which are anchored to behavioral objectives. They see PPBS devotees conjure up cost/effectiveness schemes in which precise objectives play a pivotal role. Thus they quite naturally assume that if you buy precise objectives you've also paid your first installment on the entire PPBS-accountability syndrome.

It is true that measurable instructional objectives can be highly useful in implementing schemes to satisfy the current quest for educational accountability ; yet, to organize one's instructional thinking around precise goal statements in no way commits an instructor to the whole PPBS routine. In general, there is undoubtedly a positive correlation between educators' proclivities to employ measurable objectives and their inclinations to adopt an accountability stance. Nevertheless, a teacher who wishes to employ measurable objectives can do so while eschewing all the trappings of accountability.

Objectives and Teacher Evaluation

In part because of the general movement toward accountability, we are beginning to see measurable objectives employed in procedures designed to assess a teacher's instructional skill. In several states—for example, California, Florida, and Colorado—there is considerable activity at the state legislative level to devise schemes for evaluating the quality of the state's educational enterprise in terms of specific instructional goals.

In their 1971 legislative session, California lawmakers enacted a statewide system of teacher evaluation in which each school district in the state must set up a systematic teacher appraisal system. Local districts have certain options regarding the final form of the evaluation scheme, but the new legislation stipulates that "standards of expected student progress in each area of study" be established by all districts. Many California educators are interpreting this to mean that local districts must adopt precise instructional goals stated in terms of learner behavior. Further, the new law requires that each teacher's competence be assessed (probationary teachers annually, nonprobationary teachers biennially) "as it relates to the established standards." Quite clearly, instructional objectives will play a central role in the attempts to implement the new California teacher evaluation law.[5]

Another teacher-evaluation approach of considerable potential involves the use of short-term teaching-performance tests as a vehicle for assessing one's instructional proficiency. A teaching-performance test consists of determining a teacher's ability to accomplish a pre-specified instructional objective with a small group of randomly assigned learners. By controlling the ability of learners (through both randomization and statistical adjustments) and keeping constant the instructional task (that is, the objective to be achieved), it is possible to discriminate among teachers with respect to this particular instructional skill—the ability to bring about pre-specified behavior changes in learners. At least one firm[6] is now providing a limited service to evaluate teachers according to their skill with respect to teaching-performance tests and, perhaps more importantly, is providing teaching-improvement kits designed to enhance teachers' skills on this type of instructional task. We can readily foresee the more frequent use of such measurement strategies, whereby teachers will be judged, at least in part, by their ability to help their pupils achieve both cognitive and affective instructional goals.

Objectives Plus Measures

Most classroom teachers can recount stories of an earlier era when their principal asked them to write out a list of educational objectives—typically broad goals at the platitude plateau—which were dutifully prepared, then placed in the desk drawer to be trotted forth only on PTA or back-to-school nights. Such goal statements rarely, if ever, made any difference in what went on in the classroom. But these, of course, were nonbehavioral goals that were really not supposed to affect practice, only offer solace to the public. Now, however, we find educators falling into the same trap with behavioral objectives. They believe that merely by having teachers gin up a flock of performance objectives, a moribund instructional operation will be magically transformed into pedagogical grandeur. It doesn't happen that way.

A well-stated instructional objective communicates an educator's aspiration for his learners. To assess the degree to which the objective has been achieved, we need measures based on the objectives. By providing the measures—and this certainly includes more than pencil-and-paper tests—we can make it easier for teachers to find out whether the objective has been attained. And we have to make it *easy* for teachers to live the good pedagogical life. Some religious conservatives erect hurdle after hurdle which their brethren must leap on the way to the good life. The prudent pastor makes it simple, not difficult, to live the righteous life.

Objectives with related measures can make a ton of difference in our schools. Teachers are generally well-intentioned and conscientious human beings. They want what's best for their pupils. If they discover their goals are not being achieved via current instructional strategies, they'll probably try something different. But if they only have objectives, without measures of those objectives, the odds are that they'll never find out how well their children are really doing. We desperately need more measures to match our objectives. Behavioral objectives *sans* measures offer only modest instructional advantages; behavioral objectives *with* measures can yield dramatic dividends.

Needs Assessment Enterprises

As more educators are becoming familiar with measurable instructional objectives, they are finding more uses for them, as with most new tools. One application of explicit objectives which seems particularly noteworthy involves their use in systematically deciding on the goals of an educational system, e.g., district or statewide. Stimulated largely by requirements of ESEA Title III programs which demand the conduct of an educational needs assessment in which local educational deficiencies are identified, several educators are carrying out their needs assessments by using measurable objectives. More specifically, they are either generating sets of measurable objectives or selecting them from objectives depositories, then having different clienteles, such as community representatives or students, rank the objectives in terms of their suitability for inclusion in the curriculum.

Because the use of measurable objectives reduces the ambiguity associated with statements of educational intentions, noneducators are better able to comprehend and thereby judge the importance of alternative instructional goals. By averaging the rankings of representative groups, the educational decision maker soon acquires a more enlightened estimate of the curriculum preferences of his school system's constituents.

In view of strong drives throughout the nation for legitimate community involvement in the schools, many astute school people will see the use of objective-based needs assessments as a reasonable vehicle for allowing apropriate groups to express their educational preferences. We can anticipate increased usage of objectives in this fashion.

Objectives and Evaluation

Some educators mistakenly believe that in order to conduct a defensible evaluation of an educational enterprise one must judge the degree to which the program's instructional objectives have been achieved. Michael Scriven, perhaps America's foremost evaluation theorist, has recently argued for *goal-free evaluation* in which one attends to the outcomes of an instructional sequence without any consideration whatsoever of what was intended by the instructional planners. After all, it is not the instructional designers' rhetoric to which we should attend, but to the results their designs produce. Scriven's suggestions pertain to the role of an independent evaluator who might be unduly constrained in his attention to consequences if he becomes too familiar with an instructional project's goals.

This does not suggest that an evaluation cannot be carried out in terms of project objectives, but if a *goal-based evaluation* strategy is used, then the evaluator should be certain to (1) make an assessment of the worth of the original objectives and (2) carefully search for unanticipated side effects of the instruction not encompassed by the original goal statements. As Scriven puts it, objectives may be essential for instructional planning but not necessary for certain models of educational evaluation.

Some classroom teachers who might otherwise organize a proportion of their instruction around measurable objectives have been so intimidated by behavioral-objectives zealots demanding "measurability for each objective" that they reject the entire objectives bit. It is easy to see how those people who are enamoured of rational instructional planning can get carried away in their enthusiasm for measurability. After all, if a teacher can't tell whether a goal has been achieved, how can the teacher decide whether an instructional sequence is helping or harming the pupils' achievement of the goal? Interestingly enough, most educational goals can be operationalized so that we can tease out indicators of the degree to which they have been attained. Even for long-range goals we can usually find proximate predictors which, albeit less than perfect, can give us a rough fix on the degree to which the instruction is successful.

However, many busy classroom teachers do not have the time, or perhaps the ingenuity, to carve out measurable indicators of some of their more elusive educational goals. These teachers, I believe, can be permitted to devote a certain portion of their instruction to the pursuit of highly important goals which, although unmeasurable by a given teacher, are so intrinsically praiseworthy that they merit the risk. The remainder of the teacher's instruction, however, should be organized around goals which are clear, hence clearly assessable.

In an effort to keep the reader current with respect to instructional objectives, I have attempted to skitter through a potpourri of contemporary issues regarding objectives. To me the term "potpourri" has always referred to some sort of a miscellaneous collection. I made a last-minute dictionary check as I wrote this final paragraph and discovered that Webster offers a comparable interpretation—except that the *literal* definition of "potpourri" is a "rotten pot." The reader will have to decide whether the foregoing potpourri is literal, nonliteral, or merely illiterate.

References

1. MAGER, ROBERT, *Preparing Instructional Objectives* (Belmont, Calif.: Fearon Publishers, 1962).

2. BLOOM, BENJAMIN S. *et al.*, *Taxonomy of Educational Objectives, Handbook I: Cognitive Domain* (New York: David McKay, 1956); KRATHWOHL DAVID R. *et al.*, *Taxonomy of Educational Objectives, Handbook II: Affective Domain* (New York: David McKay, 1964).

3. For example, see Hans P. Guth's tirade in *The English Journal* (September 1970, pp. 785–92), "The Monkey on the Bicycle: Behavioral Objectives and the Teaching of English." But don't pass up Peter W. Airasian's dissection of Guth's position in the April 1971 issue of the same journal (pp 495–99), "Behavioral Objectives and the Teaching of English."

4. The Laboratory of Educational Research at the University of Colorado, Boulder, for example, is setting up a pool of measures in the affective domain under Gene V. Glass's leadership.

5. For a discussion of the California teacher-evaluation law, see W. James Popham, *Designing Teacher Evaluation Systems* (Los Angeles: Instructional Objectives Exchange, 1971).

6. Instructional Appraisal Services, 105 Christopher Circle, Ithaca, N.Y., 14850; or Box 24821, Los Angeles, Calif. 90024.

3

Must All Objectives Be Behavioral?

Considerable insight can be gained about ancient man by inspecting the residual artifacts associated with his normal activities. A competent archaeologist, given a handful of potsherds and stone tools, can derive amazingly sound inferences regarding a preliterate society's life style, physical appearance, and so forth.

During recent months I have been probing my own thinking regarding instructional objectives, and have found archaeological tactics useful. Specifically, I have been examining my personal artifacts, collected during the past decade, which are particularly relevant to the question of whether instructional objectives should be stated in behavioral, that is, measurable, terms. As I share with the reader these artifacts and the inferences I derived from them, a judgment can be made regarding the adequacy of my archaeologically derived insights, and the merits of my current answer to the question, "Must *all* objectives be behavioral?"

DATE: Winter 1960.

ARTIFACT: Several used practice sheets from an early field-test version of Robert Mager's classic book on instructional objectives.

INFERENCE: These yellowed relics recall a time when I was on the faculty at San Francisco State College and Bob Mager, who lived nearby, was trying out preliminary versions of his self-instruction booklet, *Preparing Objectives for Programmed Instruction,* in my classes. For me, this was a period both of curiosity regarding the merits of measurable objectives and of increasing belief that such objectives could be useful in instruction. Having been reared during teacher education and graduate school days on a diet of grossly general objectives such as the *Seven Cardinal Principles of Secondary Education* ("Worthy use of leisure

Reprinted from the April, 1972, issue of *Educational Leadership,* Vol. 29, No. 7, p. 605.

time"), I was fascinated with what seemed to be a powerful way of clarifying a teacher's instructional intentions. Enough of gunky generalities. Precision was around the corner.

DATE: Fall 1962.
ARTIFACT: A blue and gold bumper sticker which reads *"Help Stamp Out Nonbehavioral Objectives!"*
INFERENCE: Upon joining the UCLA faculty, I had these bumper stickers printed (in UCLA colors) to distribute to my students, friends, and selected enemies. This artifact probably reflects the zenith of my zeal for behavioral objectives, the religious ardor of any recent convert being a well-established phenomenon. If students asked, "Can I use nonbehavioral objectives in my teaching?" I would respond "Certainly, but they won't be helpful."

If I found a colleague using nonbehavioral objectives for his own classes, I sneered distainfully. Since I was a new, nontenured faculty member, the degree to which my sneer was visible depended heavily on the academic rank of the colleague in question, full professors receiving only a mild upper-lip quiver.

DATE: Fall 1964.
ARTIFACT: A two-tone green bumper sticker which reads *"Help Stamp Out Nonbehavioral Objectives."*
INFERENCE: There are two noticeable differences between this relic and the 1962 artifact. First, and unimportantly, there is the color difference. This was attributable to the fact that at the same time I had exhausted the supply of blue and gold stickers I bought a green Volkswagen. I wanted a color-compatible bumper sticker. Second, and more critical, note that in this new bumper sticker *there is no exclamation point!* I can recall asking the printer to delete it from the new version, primarily to reflect my increasingly moderate stance.

DATE: Spring 1966.
ARTIFACT: A heavily marked copy of an AERA paper by Elliot Eisner entitled "Educational Objectives: Help or Hindrance."
INFERENCE: This paper was given by Elliot at an annual meeting of the American Educational Research Association. It represented the first time I had heard someone systematically attack the glories of behavioral objectives. I was aghast. I had not met Elliot previously, and I can recall standing up in the crowded meeting room after he read his paper and saying, "I have never before heard a paper with which I was in total disagreement with every point made; fortunately, this is such a paper." For

me, it was an enthralling emotional experience. This artifact marked the beginning of my combative period.

DATE: Spring 1966.

ARTIFACT: A handwritten first draft copy of a paper I wrote entitled, "Probing the Validity of Arguments Against Behavioral Objectives."

INFERENCE: It does not take a sophisticated analyst, archaeological or psychological, to infer from the title which side I was taking in what was emerging as a debate between proponents of behavioral objectives and those other villains. An inspection of the content of the paper reveals a pretty hard-line rejection of any criticism of behavioral objectives. The emergence of critics had galvanized my support of measurable objectives as a technique for educational improvement—which, if not quite panacean, were almost that praiseworthy.

DATE: Summer 1966.

ARTIFACT: An apparently unused white T-shirt with red block letters reading "Help Stamp Out Nonbehavioral Objectives."

INFERENCE: This T-shirt had been given to me by several graduate students who were aware of my opposition to nonmeasurable objectives and also of my fondness for the Southern California beaches. They pointed out that since one could secure a sunburn through the white cloth, but not the red letters, I could wear the shirt on the beach for several sunny weekends, then remove it and be a living symbol of support for behavioral objectives. The fact that the shirt appears to be unused suggests either a mellowing of my position or, probably, cowardice.

DATE: Fall 1966.

ARTIFACT: A badly scratched original filmstrip entitled *Educational Objectives*.

INFERENCE: Preparation of this filmstrip marked the peak of my evangelical period. I continued to encounter scores of educators who had not even heard of a measurable instructional objective, much less were actively using them. So I developed a filmstrip-tape program to spread the word. The half-hour program was revised nine times before being released and was able to accomplish reliably its own objectives. Perhaps in part because it has been so widely used, I now regret the choice of the expression "behavioral objective," which is employed throughout the program. Although for many people the term "behavioral" connotes some sort of mechanistic approach to instruction, such an approach is not necessarily associated with this conception of an instructional objective. Undoubtedly the choice of a phrase such as "performance objective" or "operational objective" would have been preferable.

As one surveys the general message conveyed in the filmstrip-tape program, it is almost exclusively an advocacy of measurable goals and a castigation of nonbehavioral goals "because we really can't tell what such nebulous statements mean."

DATE: Spring 1968.

ARTIFACT: The original typescript of a colloquy destined to appear in the AERA monograph, *Instructional Objectives*.

INFERENCE: A hard-liner begins to soften. This typescript was based on a February 1968 conversation among Elliot Eisner (the originator of the Spring 1966 artifact), Louise Tyler, Howard Sullivan, and myself. We had each prepared separate chapters for an AERA monograph on the topic of instructional objectives and subsequently met one long evening in a Chicago hotel room to conduct tape-recorded discussions of each of the chapters. These recordings were subsequently transcribed, edited, and later appeared in the monograph published by Rand McNally & Company in 1969.

I had become better acquainted with Elliot since our first meeting in 1966. Nevertheless, on that February evening I expected him to be a recalcitrant opponent of measurable goals. He wasn't. He was quite reasonable. A skilled archaeologist analyzing the transcript of the conversation would not be able to tell that I was thinking, "Elliot has some good points." But I was.

DATE: Fall 1968.

ARTIFACT: A handwritten proposal for the establishment of the Instructional Objectives Exchange.

INFERENCE: I was tired of hearing teachers complain they were too busy to write out measurable objectives for their instruction. It seemed that we might reasonably expect them to be selectors, not generators, of precise goals. Hence, while returning from an administrators' workshop in Fresno, I decided to try to set up an operation analogous to an "objectives bank" so that educators could draw out collections of behavioral objectives, then select those which were appropriate for their local instructional situations. The Instructional Objectives Exchange was established as a project of the UCLA Center for the Study of Evaluation later that year and is now operating as a nonprofit educational corporation. While the vast majority of objectives currently distributed by the Exchange are behaviorally stated, there are a number of general, nonbehavioral goals that are used as descriptors of large groups of more specific objectives.

DATE: Winter 1970.

ARTIFACT: A two-tone blue bumper sticker which reads *"Help Stamp Out Some Nonbehavioral Objectives!"*

INFERENCE: The floodgates may have been opened. The addition of the term "some" to the sticker indicates a putty-like softening of the former hard-liner. The reintroduction of an exclamation mark (with its already demonstrated capability of being deleted) may foreshadow even more softening in the future. In reality, when I distribute the current bumper stickers, it gives me an opportunity to describe my current thinking on the question of whether instructional objectives should be measured. A brief description of that position follows.

The Current Stance

It is probably unnecessary to observe that ten years of experience with a certain point of view have led to improvements. Nonetheless, I am going to assert that my current ideas regarding the necessity of operationality in objectives seem a great deal more defensible than my zealous exclusivism of the early 1960's.

My advocacy of measurable goals has not been altered one whit. Insofar as an instructional objective is stated with sufficient clarity that we can *measure* whether it has been achieved, then clear instruction and evaluation benefits arise. Because some of our most important educational goals are particularly elusive, we should invest greater resources in devising sophisticated measurement tactics to assess such currently unmeasurable outcomes. During recent months at the Instructional Objectives Exchange we have been constructing measurement devices to get at such educational outcomes as students' attitudes toward learning, tolerance toward minority groups, self-concept, judgment, and attitudes toward drug use. These objectives and measures are not all that polished yet, but they are better than the ones we had a few years ago.

There are many promising measurement avenues which American educators have not yet traveled with sufficient verve—that is, financial support. For example, a number of important advances have recently been made in the use of physiological indicators such as the pupil dilation of one's eyes to serve as a reliable index of interest. We cannot be satisfied with the conventional testing approaches we have lived with for years. New unobtrusive and exotic assessment schemes must be developed. Thus, point one in my current position is that we must continue to pursue measurable objectives, for our ultimate aim should still be to employ instructional objectives which permit us to tell whether they have been accomplished.

However, there are some important goals we have for our children that are *currently* unassessable. To the extent that such goals are extremely meritorious, they are *worth the risk* of our pursuing them even if we cannot reliably discern whether they have been accomplished. High-gain goals warrant high-risk instructional strategies. Let's use an illustration. Suppose our aim is to have children acquire a certain attitudinal predisposition that will be manifest, by definition, only after they become adults. Our best hope for assessment is to isolate predictor behaviors that are currently measurable and use these as proxies for the long-term goals. This is a defensible plan, *if* we can isolate proxy behaviors in which we can be confident. But since we have really just begun to get very sophisticated and circumventious in our measurement approaches, there are long-range goals for which we presently can't find suitable proxies. Accordingly, I believe that a reasonable proportion of an instructor's goals, if they are of sufficient import, can be of a nonbehavioral nature.

The magnitude of the proportion is, of course, at issue. It seems that in some content-laden classes the proportions of nonmeasurable goals might be very small. In other courses—for example, the humanities and aesthetics—the proportions might be much larger. What troubles one about ever voicing this "permit some nonmeasurable goals" point of view is that too many teachers may employ it as an excuse for business as usual, and today's business as usual in American education is unacceptable. The *overwhelming* proportion of objectives pursued by our teachers are unmeasurable, hence of little utility. It may well be that the chief deterrent to improved educational quality is that our teachers have no way of telling how well they are doing. Measurable goals permit defensible quality judgments. Nonmeasurable goals do not. Thus, to endorse the inclusion of a proportion of nonmeasurable objectives for instructional planning is not to endorse the status quo in our educational system regarding the use of instructional goals. Too few teachers employ a sufficiently large proportion of measurable objectives to be able to discern whether the bulk of the instructional efforts are satisfactory. This situation must be altered.

"Must *all* objectives be behavioral?" The answer is *no.* "Should *most* objectives be behavioral?" The answer is *yes.* It will demand far greater ingenuity and effort to produce an educational world compatible with the second answer than with the first. Hopefully, in eons to come, some archaeologist of the future will unearth our present society's educational artifacts and discern that our answers and the resulting actions were correct.

PART TWO

Curricular and Instructional Uses of Objectives

Proponents of measurable instructional objectives characteristically tout the advantages of stating precise goals for curriculum and instruction activities. The first essay in this section deals with the curricular influence of measurable objectives in a rather general fashion, and the two selections following it offer a specific application of measurable goals to the determination of what should be taught. The final essay examines instructional considerations associated with measurable objectives and includes an analysis of the typical arguments offered by opponents of measurable objectives.

4

Curriculum Control by Objective

Through the years educators have generally endorse
of deciding on objectives prior to the selection of instructio
That this should be so is not surprising, since elementary l
that one should know what is to be accomplished before
procedures to accomplish it. We might assume that, once ider.
cational objectives would have exerted considerable influer.
nature of the curriculum and classroom instructional proced
until recently this has not been so.

There are several reasons why educational objectives have
very influential in curricular and instructional decisions. The mos
nent reason has been the lack of specificity with which objectiv
been described. Through the centuries educators have stated their
tions in general terms (for example, "the learner will become qua
tively competent") that leave much room for interpretation about
specific kinds of tasks the learner will be able to perform correctly
instruction. This ambiguity has yielded both positive and negative c
sequences. On the positive side, from such general objectives as hav
been communicated to school boards, parents, and other interested lay
groups, it is possible to get a general idea of one's educational intentions.
If an educator were to delineate his instructional objectives in great
detail, he might find it difficult to communicate with members of the lay
community, particularly considering the curricular competence and available time of lay groups.

Another significant advantage of generally stated instructional
objectives, at least from the point of view of some educators, is that the
very ambiguity of global objectives makes it next to impossible for educators to be held accountable for their attainment. As long as educational

Reprinted from *Encyclopedia of Educaion*, Lee C. Deighton, Editor-in-Chief, Vol. 2, p. 575. Copyright © Crowell-Collier Educational Corporation 1971.

proclaim such glowing intentions as "the promotion of good
p," there is little that can be done to verify whether or not their
e been achieved. Business and industry, of course, have rather
dexes regarding the degree to which they have been successful.
any which fails to realize a net profit at the close of the year either
s its practices or goes bankrupt. The criteria by which we judge
ectiveness of an educational program are far more elusive. They
articularly difficult to determine when the goals for that program
tated at such a comprehensive level of generality that one cannot
y tell what they mean.

Some educators have distinguished among levels of objectives:
ntions that are held by the society in general are referred to as *aims*;
entions that are held by a school or perhaps a school district are called
als; intentions that are held by an individual teacher or team of teachers
re called *objectives*. Other writers refer to the different levels of ob-
ectives as *societal goals, institutional goals*, and *instructional goals*
(Goodlad 1966). Unfortunately, at least in view of their impact upon
the curriculum, many classroom teachers and school districts have
specified their objectives at a level of generality more appropriate for
communicating with the society at large than with those who must
decide upon the nature of the curriculum.

One prominent disadvantage associated with broadly stated goals
is that the multiple interpretations possible for a particular objective have
made it extremely difficult to devise relevant measures of whether or not
the objective has been achieved. It is highly unlikely, for example, that
a large group of educators would agree upon how best to measure the
following objective: "The student will understand the meaning of Shake-
speare's most significant passages." Because of the difficulty of reaching
consensus regarding the manner in which to measure such generally
stated goals, diverse measures of an objective's attainment have been
employed, and educational evaluation has almost been reduced to a
"pay your money and choose your method" approach.

In much the same way, loose objectives have contributed im-
measurably to the diverse array of curricular content seen in the United
States. Because there has been no clear agreement as to how a particular
objective was to be achieved, instructional activities have often been
based on such criteria as the manner in which a discipline outlined its
content. Rarely has a curriculum really been limited by its objectives.
The curriculum maker's question through the decades has not been
"What learning activities will most efficiently promote the attainment
of these particular objectives?" Rather, the curriculum maker has asked,

"What content should this course cover?" The covering of content, which exposes the student to certain concepts, usually lacks a consideration of objectives (that is, what the learner will be able to do) and thus, has led to a form of curricular decision making which has been essentially unrelated to the nature of instructional goals.

Many curriculum planners, such as individuals at the school district level and teachers in the classroom, have often identified their objectives *after* having decided on what to do in the class. The first question that such curriculum planners ask is invariably "What will we have the students do?" The question "How will the objectives be achieved?" is rarely, if ever, raised.

How are new curricula devised? Unfortunately, an all-too-common practice in public education has been the devising of curricula for school districts by cutting and pasting from curriculum guides issued by other districts. Until recent years, we had seldom seen systematic efforts to develop a rationale for helping educators select effective curricular materials.

Although for a number of years a handful of curriculum specialists (Tyler 1950) had been advising educators first to specify objectives precisely, then to design instructional sequences, and finally to determine whether or not the objectives had been achieved through the use of these sequences, few American educators followed their advice. The post-Sputnik era brought a greater concern about the quality of American education and, as a consequence, there emerged several national curriculum projects. Even these curriculum reform programs usually fell short of the mark with respect to the degree of specificity required for useful objectives. To have much of a controlling effect upon the quality of the curriculum that ensues from it, an objective must be stated very explicitly. Perhaps because the leaders of the curriculum reform projects were often leaders in their academic disciplines rather than instructional specialists, objectives emerging from national curriculum projects were too often those of a content-coverage nature.

Since the early 1960's there has been considerable ferment in American education regarding the manner in which instructional objectives should be stated. As a consequence, concern has increased over the influence that objectives have upon the curriculum. Owing in large measure to developments in the field of programmed instruction, educators have become increasingly aware of the desirability of stating their instructional objectives in terms of desired modifications in learner behavior. There has been an increasing tendency among educators to eschew the usual techniques of describing objectives in very loose terms

("The student will appreciate my subject"), in terms of content coverage ("This course will cover the important events of the U.S. Civil War"), or in terms of what the teacher is to do ("The teacher will describe the critical elements of various literary forms"). Instead, instructors are now being urged to specify their objectives in terms of desired post-instruction learner behavior. Such operationally stated objectives, often referred to as behavioral objectives, offer the promise of making great impact on the nature of curriculum and instruction.

An operationally stated objective (that is, one which describes how the learner is supposed to behave after instruction) offers the ready possibility of assessing the degree to which the learner can actually behave that way. This permits an educator to determine the efficacy of a given instructional sequence and an instructor to select relevant instructional activities. Consider the following behaviorally stated objective: "The student will be able to provide oral English translations of previously unencountered simple sentences in Portuguese." It is likely that with such a behavioral objective the instructor will be able to select instructional activities which are germane to the attainment of the objective, although he could, of course, mistakenly assign activities within the general field of the study of Portuguese that would be irrelevant to the accomplishment of the objective. However, the greater the precision with which the objective is explicated, the more likely it is that the objective will permit accurate inferences regarding relevant learning activities. In this case, an examination of the objective suggests pertinent activities, such as providing the student with opportunities to practice translating previously unencountered Portuguese sentences.

Thus, one result of describing objectives in more precise language is that those objectives can be expected to exert influence on the instructional and evaluative behavior of teachers. Similar influence may be exerted on curricular decisions made by those in a position to decide what curricular elements should be selected by the schools.

There have been several other potentially important developments concerning operationally stated objectives and their impact upon the curriculum. One of these is the national assessment of educational progress (Tyler 1965), the principal aim of which has been to provide meaningful indexes of educational achievement in the United States. Initialiy, agreement was sought on a series of objectives for important areas of education, such as verbal and quantitative skills (for example, adding, subtracting, solving story problems). Having established agreement regarding desirable goals, the organization conducting the assessment of educational progress used items based on the agreed-upon objectives to measure pupils throughout the nation. Learner competencies at specified age levels were measured by an item-sampling technique (different schools and different pupils completed different items) that was both economical and deliberately designed to counteract the notion that this was a national testing program. Although it would be impossible, for example, to compare one school district with another since different test items have been used, this national assessment program will undoubtedly have some curricular impact in many schools. If for no other reasons than the clarity and dissemination of its objectives, the program will influence the kinds of objectives selected by school districts. This would seem to be one of those situations in which clarity exerts a coercive influence. We can expect school district officials to take their cues from the consensus position of experts and lay authorities so that district objectives may very likely be more congruent with the clearly articulated objectives of the national assessment program. This is not really surprising, nor is it necessarily undesirable.

Another development has been the establishment of national agencies or banks from which school districts can select objectives and related criterion items. One such agency is the Instructional Objectives Exchange, a project of the Center for the Study of Evaluation, University of California, Los Angeles. This scheme, designed to make it more practical for school districts to base their instruction upon precisely stated objectives, does not prevent the teacher from specifying his own objectives but makes it possible for him to select from objectives already prepared if he wishes. The teacher receives a pool of related criterion items with each objective selected; these items make it relatively simple to assess the degree to which an objective has been achieved. Although even behaviorally stated objectives can be used as window dressing for instruction as usual, the availability of criterion items that measure the precisely described objectives would seem likely to reduce this possibility.

The movement toward the greater influence of instructional objectives represents a predictable outgrowth of increased concern regarding educational intentions. Objectives plus measurement items may very likely influence curriculum and instructional decisions to a far greater extent than is currently the case. This trend promises to have a beneficial effect on educational practice.

How would an instructional system function if it were primarily influenced by the educational objectives it was designed to accomplish? Since the overriding focus of this form of instruction would be on the learner's attainment of specified behavioral goals and since the objective (that is, the intended behavior change in the learner) would always be the criterion for determining the efficacy of instruction, all important decisions would be made in relation to the criterion. This preoccupation with the criterion has caused such objective-oriented systems to be described as criterion-referenced.

The first step in a criterion-referenced instructional sequence is to make completely certain that the instructional objectives are stated with sufficient clarity so that there can be no ambiguity in the nature of the desired learner behavior. If there is more than one possible interpretation of how the learner will manifest achievement of the objective, such ambiguity must be eliminated. Usually the proportion of learners (for example, 90 percent) expected to achieve the objective will also be identified in advance.

After all objectives have been stated in proper operational form, the next step in criterion-referenced instruction is the development of a pool of items that will measure the achievement of the objectives. Here, the term "item" refers to any form of evaluative device, not only to paper-and-pencil measures. If feasible, there should be several items prepared for all objectives. These items, though not identical to the evaluation measures delimited by the operationally stated objective, should be drawn from the same class.

Next, for each objective several items are randomly drawn (to avoid bias) from the item pool and administered to learners prior to instruction. This pre-testing operation is necessary to establish clearly, before instruction occurs, that the learners cannot already perform what the instructor is attempting to accomplish. Untold hours of instructional time are wasted in teaching learners to do that which they are already able to do. If it is revealed that the learners already possess the intended competencies, then other objectives should obviously be selected.

If, however, the learners do not display the desired competencies, then the criterion-referenced instructor designs a sequence of instruction to promote the competencies. Because he has a clear idea of how the learner should behave following instruction, he concentrates his efforts on producing this type of behavior during the instructional sequence. If preliminary behaviors, called en route skills, must be mastered by the learner prior to acquisition of the terminal behavior, then these en route behaviors will also have to be identified and developed before the learner attempts to master the terminal behavior.

Generally, a criterion-referenced instructional sequence will provide the learners with ample opportunities to practice the behavior called for by the instructional objective. That is, the learner will be given, prior to the close of instruction, chances to behave in precisely the manner called for by the criterion. Of course, this does not mean that the learner will be given questions identical to those he must master on a final examination; instead, he will receive similar practice questions drawn from the class of those items delimited by the objective.

Since the intended criterion is clearly in mind, the criterion-referenced instructor can then employ a simple, yet powerful, tactic: he can, before instruction is concluded, check to see how many learners have mastered the criterion. This criterion check can be easily administered by randomly drawing unused items from the item pool, forming a new test, then seeing how many students display mastery of the criterion. The advantages of this criterion check should be clear. It permits the instructor to determine which learners have not yet achieved mastery of the criterion while there is still time to do something about it. He can now try to bring them up to mastery, probably by using a modification of the instructional scheme he originally employed. For those who display mastery, he can provide supplementary activities directed toward additional goals.

After the additional instruction which follows the criterion check, unused items from the item pool are administered as the final criterion test. Learner performance on this criterion test indicates whether or not the instructional sequence has been successful. If the anticipated proportion of learners achieve the criterion behaviors, the instructional sequence is considered adequate. If fewer than the anticipated proportion of learners display mastery of the criterion, the sequence is judged deficient. The important point is that any assessment of instructional proficiency is made exclusively on the ends produced by the instruction, not on the basis of the means employed.

This all-consuming commitment to achievement of objectives with a criterion-referenced strategy can be expected to result in an educational environment where objectives do indeed control the nature of the curriculum. Such a relationship between objectives and curriculum would seem to offer the hope of improved educational practice.

References

GOODLAD, JOHN I., *The Development of a Conceptual System for Dealing with Problems of Curriculum and Instruction* (Washington, D.C.: U.S. Department of Health, Education, and Welfare, 1966).

TYLER, RALPH W., *Basic Principles of Curriculum and Instruction: Syllabus for Education 360* (Chicago: The University of Chicago Press, 1950).

———, "Assessing the Progress of Education." *Phi Delta Kappan* 47, No. 1, 1965.

5

The Vanishing Curriculum Specialist:
A Proposal To Retard His Imminent
Extinction

Who is the "curriculum specialist"? What does he do? How should he be trained? Perhaps most important in the current state of American education, does he have a chance to survive?

We could, of course, commence an examination of these questions by initiating one of those delightful, uninsightful debates about whether curriculum specialists should consider the realm of instruction within their empire. Most of us have witnessed one or more of these means/ends debates, with one group of proponents arguing that curriculum folk should attend exclusively to questions regarding the *ends* of education, that is, goals or objectives. Their adversaries opine with equal conviction that a curriculum specialist should be equally attentive to the *means* of education, to wit, the instructional procedures employed to promote the attainment of certain ends.

Now it would be interesting to conduct a simple correlational analysis of (a) the manner in which curriculum professors title their basic courses and (b) their views regarding this issue. One suspects that the professor satisfied with calling his course "Basic Principles of Curriculum" is probably a member of the ends-and-means camp, while instructors of "Basic Principles of Curriculum and Instruction" offerings may feel they need to tag on the "and instruction" phrase to open up the consideration of instructional process. Now I am not proposing this investigation as a graduate level research project, although one suspects that graduate degrees in the field of curriculum have been awarded for less spectacular inquiries.

For purposes of the discussion, however, I want to set aside the question of whether a curriculum specialist should tussle with instructional means, and instead focus on his role in determining the ends of education. At the moment I am not taking sides in the "ends only" or "ends plus means" debate, but only considering that part of the curricu-

This article is based on a presentation to the Curriculum Study Group at the annual conference of the American Educational Research Association, New York, February, 1971.

lum worker's activities that are directed toward decisions regarding what the goals of an educational system ought to be.

For too many years curriculum specialists have been living off the intellectual capital originally generated by the work of such fine thinkers as Ralph Tyler and Franklin Bobbitt. Perhaps it is misleading to call people like Tyler curriculum theorists, for their suggestions were often motivated by very practical concerns. Yet, if we can contrast *theory* with *technology*, the latter being focused on a practical system of carrying out certain decision-making operations, Tyler's curricular writings fall closer to theory than technology.

Surely it is wise, as Tyler recommended, to consider alternative objectives that might be generated from a consideration of the learner, the society, and the subject discipline. Surely it is sensible, as he suggested, to appraise such objectives by screening them through a philosophy of education and a psychology of learning. These are good things to do, and we have been reminded by a number of outstanding curricular theorists that this is what curriculum workers should be doing.

I have always believed that if an individual is charged with identifying a set of defensible educational objectives he will do so more intelligently by using some systematic scheme, such as the Tyler Rationale, than by spinning them off the top of his head. A systematic rationale forces one to employ a greater degree of circumspection than would normally be the case. Yet, a personal anecdote will reveal some misgivings I have always had about the Tyler Rationale and comparable curriculum-determination schemes.

For a number of years I have taught a course for prospective secondary school teachers entitled "Curriculum and Instruction for the Secondary School." (Incidentally, no inference should be made regarding *my* stance on the ends/means debate, for it was an inherited course title.) For most of the students this is their first education course and, since it is a required course in the credential sequence, the students are obliged to complete it. Now an examination of the course title reveals that both curriculum *and* instruction are to be treated in the course. Most people would suggest that I should logically start the course with a consideration of curriculum, then turn to instruction. It seems reasonable to isolate the goals of an educational system (curriculum), then attempt to accomplish them (instruction). I agree with this logic, but I just couldn't do it; I couldn't start my course with the curriculum component. It would have confirmed my students' well-nurtured expectations that education courses were largely worthless and offered little of practical utility to the would-be teacher. I couldn't run the risk of losing my students so early in the course by transmitting that pile of generalities we call curriculum theory. Instead, I turned to the topic of instruction where there is an increasing arsenal of practical competencies that can be transmitted to prospective teachers, tangible skills that at face value appear relevant even for the beginning education student, to a teacher's instructional tasks. Only after I believed the class had accepted the worth of the course dared I introduce them to the esoteric mysteries of "the curriculum."

Unlike many fields where early theoretical advances have stimulated the growth of a full-blown technology that offers alternative answers to "How to do it?" questions, curriculum workers have apparently been content to roam in theoretical groves. How many times, for example, have we seen efforts to *operationalize* the general cues contained in the curriculum schemes of Tyler, Taba, and others? How much more common, for instance, do we find general treatises on the curriculum, with no explicit, step-by-step recommendations for their implementation.

It was small wonder that the major curriculum development projects so prevalent in recent years, to the chagrin of the curriculum specialists, called on so few members of their fraternity. "Curricularists" had precious little to offer these projects, beyond whatever native intelligence they brought to the situation. Directors of these curriculum projects needed technical help regarding the specifics of goal identification. Curriculum experts offered them only wisdom of a generalized nature. This they already had. In other words, the curriculum specialist possessed no unique competencies, only glossy generalities, which he could bring to bear on the task faced by these curriculum builders. It is small wonder that the bearers of such pearls were treated as swine.

And now, if the tenants of the Curriculum Ranch will but look around they will see that there are brigands in their barnyard. Probably as a consequence of their dereliction, there are other people starting to play the goal-determination game. Let's see who these new players are.

First, there are the omnivorous evaluation boys. Led by a staunch group of new-think evaluators, principally Egon Guba and Daniel Stuffle-beam, this expanding group of individuals has a far more expansive view of evaluation than we have historically given to this specialty. For not only does this new breed of evaluators consider their province to include (1) outcome evaluation ("product evaluation" in their language) but also (2) initial advice regarding what kind of instructional treatment to select ("input evaluation") and (3) how that treatment is working after it has been installed ("process evaluation"). More importantly, as far as the curriculum specialist is concerned, they have also undertaken (4) "context evaluation," which includes an appraisal of an extant educational situation in order to determine which instructional goals ought to be selected. These four types of evaluation constitute the Guba-Stuffle-beam CIPP model (CIPP stands for context, input, process, product), which is primarily conceived as an aid to educational decision making at all points of the instructional continuum. CIPP and comparable models are gaining increasing popularity among those who profess to be evaluation specialists.

Just because these new types of evaluators are apparently poaching on the curriculum worker's game preserve, the curriculum specialist should not be inclined to whine, "We were here first." Nevertheless, it should be noted that if curriculum people don't shape up our own house quickly, someone else is apt to do it.

As an aside, I wish to note that I am not so concerned about the apparent territorial intrusions of the CIPP-type evaluators, for if these people can do a better job at deciding what instructional goals ought to be pursued, then education will clearly benefit. What bothers me is that skilled outcome-evaluation specialists are badly needed to assess the worth of an apparently endless stream of educational decision-making including avenues previously left to other specialists—that is, (1) context evaluation in lieu of curriculum, and (2) input and process evaluation rather than instruction. In a period when truly competent educational specialists are scarce, it doesn't seem like a prudent division of labor to have evaluators take over the whole circus. On the other hand, if their aspirations can stimulate curriculum workers to produce a functional technology, then the final result will indeed be good.

Another group with curricular aspirations are the needs-assessment personnel, found primarily in projects supported by ESEA Title III funds. As a required phase of these programs, all state Title III programs have been obliged to conduct educational needs assessments in order to determine which learner needs should be ameliorated. Putting it another way, by assessing educational needs in a state or local district, the most important instructional objectives can be isolated. Because needs assessments have been required, we should not be surprised that they have been carried out. But what may come as a surprise is that in order to carry out the best goal determinations that their resources permit, many of these Title III workers are really trying to systematize what they are doing. And although we might expect such individuals to draw on the expertise of curriculum specialists, it won't be long before curriculum people have to take lessons from the individuals conducting these needs assessments. The Title III people are carrying out needs assessments on such a large scale that they have to get practical in conducting them.

Unless the curriculum specialists can evolve and sharpen a practical technology to permit better goal selection, then they ought to retire to some academic Sun City, for they are clearly ready for a pension (perhaps unearned). Other people will have done the job that should have been accomplished long ago. Back when there were no competitors, the task seemed less urgent. There are competitors now.

What might this curriculum technology look like? How would it work? In general, it must contain one or more step-by-step procedures for deciding on the goals for an educational system. The remainder of this paper will offer one illustration, albeit embryonic, of how a curriculum technology might function.

An Illustrative Curriculum Technology

In the past, one difficulty facing the person who must decide how to select educational goals was that he had few raw materials with which to work other than some general pronouncements from esteemed commissions regarding what ought to be taught. Now, however, there are new materials available which permit some different strategies. I have in mind an increasing number of collections of precisely stated, measurable instructional objectives and related test measures, such as the numerous sets of objectives and measures distributed by the Instructional Objectives Exchange. For example, one of the collections in the exchange deals with mathematics, grades 4 to 6. It includes 233 objectives plus four test items for each objective. Other collections of objectives in the affective domain present groups of objectives and measures dealing with the learner's self-concept and his attitudes toward school.

Let's briefly see how Ralph Tyler's Rationale might be practically implemented by capitalizing on these pools of objectives. First, groups of individuals should be identified who are suitable representatives of Tyler's three goal sources—the learner, the society, and the subject discipline. For example, if the task were to select objectives for mathematics (and this, of course, assumes that we are attempting only to decide on mathematics objectives, not the entire range of possible goals), then to represent the subject discipline we might identify a representative group of twenty mathematics teachers and twenty university mathematicians. To represent the society we could select twenty parents, ten businessmen, and ten elected public officials. To represent the learner we might choose forty pupils at the appropriate age range under consideration. Each of these groups could then be presented with a set of measurable mathematics objectives and asked to rate the importance of each objective on a five-point scale (5 points if the objective is extremely important, 1 point if it is extremely unimportant), with respect to whether it should be included in the curriculum. The use of item and person sampling techniques, in which different people rate only a small segment of each set of objectives, would permit each rater to consider only a manageable number of objectives, not an unwieldy collection of several hundred. We could then average the ratings of the various groups to obtain a set of data such as those presented in Table 1. Note that the mean ratings of certain objectives seem to warrant their inclusion in the curriculum. But, as we shall see, there are other considerations.

Having used Tyler's three goal sources, we can now apply his philosophic screen by explicitly weighting the mean preferences of the different rating groups according to our values regarding the importance of each group's role in deciding on the school's objectives. For example, if we considered the rankings of subject specialists to be worth twice as much as the other two groups, then we could weight the learner, society, and subject ratings .25, .25, and .50 respectively. After weighting the sources in this way, the ranking of preferred objectives is altered and objective Number 1 changes place with objective Number 4, because of the heavily weighted subject specialists' 3.5 rating of objective Number 1. With more groups involved, of course, these weighting considerations would have to be far more sophisticated. For example, we might use ratings from several separately weighted groups to yield a composite estimate from any of the three sources.

Still using a philosophical screen, we could obtain from various groups their preferences regarding the degree of desired proficiency that students should display on the highly ranked objectives. For example, for a certain kind of mathematics objective, what percentage of the intended learners should achieve what percentage correct? Thus, each highly ranked objective could have a desired proficiency level, such as 90-90, 80-80, 80-50, and so on. Deciding how well we want learners to do is a pretty subjective operation at the moment, and although there are pertinent data which could be called on, for example, prior performance levels of typical learners, this operation might also be considered to fall within a philosophical screening activity.

Turning to the psychological screen, we can undertake two procedures which might be helpful. First, we could use criterion-referenced

TABLE 1
Fictitious Mean Rating Data

Objective Number	Learners	Society Representatives	Subject Specialists	Rank
1	2.1	2.4	3.5	3
2	4.2	4.3	3.9	1
3	1.4	3.1	2.2	4
4	3.3	3.3	2.6	2
etc.				

test measures based on the highly ranked objectives to determine the learner's current status with respect to these goals. The discrepancy between the desired levels of performance and the actual levels of performance provide another useful kind of data. The importance of these discrepancies in ultimately deciding on objectives undoubtedly falls within the philosophical arena. For example, in choosing alternative objectives, should a higher ranked objective for which there is a smaller discrepancy be selected rather than a lower ranked objective for which there is a larger discrepancy? Someone has to decide. If quantitative weightings can be assigned to the relative import of (1) preference rankings and (2) discrepancies, all the better.

Another type of psychological screening activity could involve instructional psychologists who would be asked to rate the highly ranked objectives in relationship to their likelihood that they could be efficiently achieved. Putting it another way, estimates could be secured from competent psychologists regarding which objectives could be achieved with the available resources of time, money, materials, staff, and so forth. These ratings could also be built into the decision-making matrix, assigning them as much weight as would seem appropriate.

Even though this illustrative operation has been sketchily described, it is hoped that its essential ingredients reflect how a step-by-step scheme for deciding upon curriculum goals might be put together. The degree of sophistication rests with the ingenuity and resources of those devising the procedures.

It is clear that there are all sorts of different techniques that may be used to implement a goal-determination strategy. Fortunately, the efficacy of many of these alternative procedures can be determined empirically. Minor, yet non-trivial questions, such as the nature of the ranking forms that should be distributed to the various reference groups, can be answered by experimental investigations where the criterion might be stability over time of preferences by the raters in response to different types of forms. Many such issues could be resolved by the masters and doctoral theses of curriculum candidates who could now be directed to systematically expand the technology of their field.

The availability of a curriculum technology would result in many changes, particularly regarding the training of curriculum specialists. No longer would the aspiring curriculum worker emerge from his curriculum courses merely "sensitized" to the important considerations of his field. He would know how to do something that other people couldn't do. He would possess a demonstrable set of competencies. Most important of all, he would be able to use these skills to help select defensible educational objectives. This is what curriculum people have always been supposed to be able to do.

6

Objectives and Instruction

Surely one of the more interesting research questions during the past one-half century has concerned the assessment of instructional effectiveness. Innumerable investigators have attempted, through a variety of procedures, to produce defensible indices of teaching quality. . . . With few exceptions, teacher effectiveness researchers have attempted to employ means-related models in their assessment of instructional quality. Frequently, for example, the researcher has attempted to observe the teacher in action, employing rating scales which range from the simplistic to the hypersophisticated, in order to judge if the instructional procedures employed by the teacher were "good." Whether the observation schedule yielded a single overall measure or multidimensional indices of proficiency, the results have been extremely confusing. In their comprehensive review of teacher effectiveness research during the first fifty years of this century, Morsh and Wilder (1954) observed that no single teaching act was invariably associated with increased pupil performance. It has become increasingly clear that in order to judge one's teaching proficiency, there must be a consideration of such factors as the particular teacher, the particular collection of pupils, the instructional environment, and the nature of the educational goals. In other words, an instructional situation is generally so idiosyncratic that it is impossible to focus on the general quality of instructional means used by different teachers. Diverse teachers may be able to employ markedly different means and yet achieve precisely the same ends with equal efficiency. Our assessment of teaching competence, therefore, should be based on the instructor's ability to achieve desired ends; and should not relate at all to his use of particular means.

A series of investigations designed to assess the validity of a new approach to the assessment of instructional quality has recently been reported (Popham and Baker, 1966). In these investigations a teacher was given a set of explicit instructional goals stated in terms of measurable learning behavior. In addition, possible learning activities and resource materials were supplied for the teacher. The teacher's task was to accomplish the prespecified instructional ends, using whatever means he wished. Pre-test and post-test pupil examinations, based exclusively on the given instructional objectives, were used to assess the teacher's ability to accomplish the goals. That is, by providing a constant set of objectives it was possible to contrast the ability of different teachers to achieve those goals through the use of whatever instructional procedures they preferred.

Early attempts to validate these "performance tests of teaching proficiency" are worth mentioning. The initial contention of the investigators was that experienced teachers would teach better using these kinds of performance tests than "people off the street." In other words, it seemed reasonable that experienced teachers ought to be able to out-perform nonteachers in promoting learner achievement to prespecified instructional objectives. Accordingly, several investigations were conducted (Popham, 1967b) comparing the performance of experienced teachers with housewives and college students, none of whom had any teaching experience. None of these investigations revealed a significant difference favoring the experienced teachers. The investigators concluded that experienced teachers are simply not more experienced at accomplishing prespecified behavior changes in learners.

There undoubtedly must be training provided for teachers so that they acquire the skills necessary to efficiently achieve such behavior changes. Indeed, it has been suggested that if teacher education institutions cannot demonstrate that they can markedly increase the teacher's ability to bring about such behavior changes in learners, they either should modify their teacher preparation programs or close up shop.

A related investigation was reported by Baker (1967) in which a series of behavioral objectives and nonbehavioral objectives were presented to teachers. The behavioral objectives were drawn (both by random procedures and by the judgment of instructional experts) from sets of behavioral objectives which could be inferred from the nonbehavioral objectives. For example, if the nonbehavioral objective ran as follows: "The student will understand the nature of social science research hypotheses," a set of five operational statements which could reflect this competency were described. From these five behavioral statements, objectives were drawn for the behavioral objective teacher groups. Comparisons were then made of the ability of teachers to achieve these objectives (behavioral or nonbehavioral) during a two-hour instructional period. No differences in the performance of the teachers using behavioral objectives and those using nonbehavioral objectives were detected on related test measures.

An interesting explanation of these results was based, in part, on a questionnaire which the investigator administered to the teachers using behavioral objectives. After the instructional period had been completed, they were asked to judge the relevance of test items to the objectives they had been given. The teachers who had been supplied with precise objectives were unable to exceed chance levels of performance in judging whether test items were relevant to the objectives they had been given. The investigator concluded that the teachers' inability to identify relevant test items probably reflected their general incapability of coping instructionally with precise objectives. The suggestion was made that the experienced teacher is not experienced in dealing with precisely specified objectives and must be trained to do so.

The Threat-Potential of Precision*

Notwithstanding apparently cogent arguments in favor of precise objectives, most educators have been inordinately successful in avoiding them. In the remaining paragraphs ten reasons will be examined which educators employ to escape the practice of stating their objectives behaviorally. Each of the reasons has been advocated in print or in public meetings. Each reason has its own degree or reasonableness or emotionality. Each reason carries its own peculiar appeal to different sorts of educators. Each reason is essentially invalid. Following each, an attempt will be made to refute the objection contained in or implied by that reason.

Reason one: Trivial learner behaviors are the easiest to operationalize, hence the really important outcomes of education will be under-emphasized.

This particular objection to the use of precise goals is frequently voiced by educators who have recently become acquainted with the procedures for stating explicit, behavioral objectives. Since even behavioral objectives enthusiasts admit that the easiest kinds of pupil behaviors to operationalize are usually the most pedestrian, it is not surprising to find so many examples of behavioral objectives which deal with the picayune. In spite of its overall beneficial influence, the programmed

*The remaining paragraphs are based on symposium presentations at the 19th Annual Conference on Educational Research, California Advisory Council on Educational Research, San Diego, California, November 16, 1967 and at the annual meeting of the American Educational Research Association, Chicago, Illinois, February 8–10, 1968.

book by Robert Mager (1962) dealing with the preparation of instructional objectives has probably suggested to many that precise objectives are usually trivial. Almost all of Mager's examples deal with cognitive behaviors which, according to Bloom's *Taxonomy*, would be identified at the very lowest level.

Contrary to the objection raised in reason one, however, the truth is that explicit objectives make it far *easier* for educators to attend to *important* instructional outcomes. To illustrate, if you were to ask a social science teacher what his objectives were for his government class, and he responded as follows, "I want to make my students better citizens so that they can function effectively in our nation's dynamic democracy," you would probably find little reason to fault him. His objective sounds so profound and eminently worthwhile that few could criticize it. Yet, beneath such facades of profundity, many teachers really are aiming at extremely trivial kinds of pupil behavior changes. How often, for example, do we find "good citizenship" measured by a trifling true-false test? Now if we'd asked for the teacher's objectives in operational terms and had discovered that, indeed, all the teacher was really attempting to do was promote the learner's achievement on a true-false test, we might have rejected the aim as being unimportant. But this is possible *only* with the precision of explicitly stated goals.

In other words, there is the danger that because of their ready translation to operational statements, teachers will tend to identify too many trivial behaviors as goals. But the very fact that we can make these behaviors explicit permits the teacher and his colleagues to scrutinize them carefully and thus eliminate them as unworthy of our educational efforts. Instead of encouraging unimportant outcomes in education, the use of explicit instructional objectives makes it possible to identify and reject those objectives which are unimportant.

Reason two: Prespecification of explicit goals prevents the teacher from taking advantage of instructional opportunities unexpectedly occurring in the classroom.

When one specifies explicit *ends* for an instructional program there is no necessary implication that the *means* to achieve those ends are also specified. Serendipity in the classroom is always welcome, but, and here is the important point, *it should always be justified in terms of its contribution to the learner's attainment of worthwhile objectives.* Too often teachers may believe they are capitalizing on unexpected instructional opportunities in the classroom, whereas measurement of pupil growth toward any defensible criterion would demonstrate that what has happened is merely ephemeral entertainment for the pupils, temporary diversion, or some other irrelevant classroom event.

Prespecification of explicit goals does not prevent the teacher from taking advantage of unexpectedly occurring instructional opportunities in the classroom, it only tends to make the teacher justify these spontaneous learning activities in terms of worthwhile instructional ends. There are undoubtedly gifted teachers who can capitalize magnificently on the most unexpected classroom events. These teachers should not be restricted from doing so. But the teacher who prefers to probe instructional periphery, just for the sake of its spontaneity, should be deterred by the prespecification of explicit goals.

Reason three: Besides pupil behavior changes, there are other types of educational outcomes which are important, such as changes in parental attitudes, the professional staff, community values, etc.

There are undoubtedly some fairly strong philosophic considerations associated with this particular reason. It seems reasonable that there are desirable changes to be made in our society which might be undertaken by the schools. Certainly, we would like to bring about desirable modifications in such realms as the attitudes of parents. But as a number of educational philosophers have reminded us, the schools cannot be all things to all segments of society. It seems that the primary responsibility of the schools should be to educate effectively the youth of the society. To the extent that this is so, all modifications of parental attitudes, professional staff attitudes, etc., should be weighed in terms of a later measurable impact on the learner himself. For example, the school administrator who tells us he wishes to bring about new kinds of attitudes on the part of his teachers should ultimately have to demonstrate that these modified attitudes result in some kind of desirable learner changes. To stop at merely modifying the behavior of teachers, without demonstrating further effects upon the learner, would be insufficient.

So while we can see that there are other types of important social outcomes to bring about, it seems that the school's primary responsibility is to its pupils. Hence, all modifications in personnel or external agencies should be justified in terms of their contribution toward the promotion of desired pupil behavior changes.

Reason four: Measurability implies behavior which can be objectively, mechanistically measured, hence there must be something dehumanizing about the approach.

This fourth reason is drawn from a long history of resistance to measurement on the grounds that it must, of necessity, reduce human learners to quantifiable bits of data. This resistance probably is most strong regarding earlier forms of measurement which were almost exclusively examination-based, and were frequently multiple-choice test measures at that. But a broadened conception of evaluation suggests that there are diverse and extremely sophisticated ways of securing qualitative as well as quantitative indices of learner performance.

One is constantly amazed to note the incredible agreement among a group of judges assigned to evaluate the complicated gyrations of skilled springboard divers in the televised reports of national aquatic championships. One of these athletes will perform an exotic, twisting dive and a few seconds after he has hit the water five or more judges raise cards reflecting their independent evaluations which can range from 0 to 10. The five ratings very frequently run as follows: 7.8, 7.6, 7.7, 7.8, and 7.5. The possibility of reliably judging something as qualitatively complicated as a springboard dive does suggest that our measurement procedures do not have to be based on a theory of reductionism. It is currently possible to assess many complicated human behaviors in a refined fashion. Developmental work is under way in those areas where we now must rely on primitive measures.

Reason five: It is somehow undemocratic to plan in advance precisely how the learner should behave after instruction.

This particular reason was raised a few years ago in a professional journal (Arnstine, 1964) suggesting that the programmed instruction movement was basically undemocratic because it spelled out in advance how the learner was supposed to behave after instruction. A brilliant refutation (Komisar and McClellan, 1965) appeared several months later in which the rebutting authors responded that instruction is by its very nature undemocratic and to imply that freewheeling democracy is always present in the classroom would be untruthful. Teachers generally have an idea of how they wish learners to behave, and they promote these goals with more or less efficiency. Society knows what it wants its young to become, perhaps not with the precision we would desire, but certainly in general. And if the schools were allowing students to "democratically" deviate from societally mandated goals, one can be sure that the institutions would cease to receive society's approbation and support.

Reason six: That isn't really the way teaching is; teachers rarely specify their goals in terms of measurable learner behaviors; so let's set realistic expectations of teachers.

Jackson (1966) recently offered this argument. He observed that teachers just don't specify their objectives in terms of measurable learner behavior and implied that, since this is the way the real world is, we ought to recognize it and live with it. Perhaps.

There is obviously a difference between identifying the status quo and applauding it. Most of us would readily concede that few teachers specify their instructional aims in terms of measurable learner behaviors; *but they should.* What we have to do is to mount a widespread campaign to modify this aspect of teacher behavior. Instructors must begin to identify their instructional intentions in terms of measurable learner behaviors. The way teaching really is at the moment just isn't good enough.

Reason seven: In certain subject areas, e.g., fine arts and the human-
ities, it is more difficult to identify measurable pupil behaviors.

Sure it's tough. Yet, because it is difficult in certain subject fields
to identify measurable pupil behaviors, those subject specialists should
not be allowed to escape this responsibility. Teachers in the fields of art
and music often claim that it is next to impossible to identify acceptable
works of art in precise terms, but they do it all the time. In instance after
instance the art teacher does make a judgment regarding the acceptability
of pupil-produced artwork. What the art teacher is reluctant to do is put
his evaluative criteria on the line. He has such criteria. He must have to
make his judgments. But he is loath to describe them in terms that anyone
can see.

Any English teacher, for example, will tell you how difficult it is
to make a valid judgment of a pupil's essay response. Yet criteria lurk
whenever this teacher does make a judgment, and these criteria must be
made explicit. No one who really understands education has ever argued
that instruction is a simple task. It is even more difficult in such areas as
the arts and humanities. As a noted art educator observed several years
ago, art educators must quickly get to the business of specifying "tentative, but clearly defined criteria" by which they can judge their learners'
artistic efforts (Munro, 1960).

Reason eight: While loose general statements of objectives may
appear worthwhile to an outsider, if most educational goals were stated
precisely, they would be revealed as generally innocuous.

This eighth reason contains a great deal of potential threat for
school people. The unfortunate truth is that much of what is going on
in the schools today is indefensible. Merely to reveal the nature of some
of the behavior changes we are bringing about in our schools would be
embarrassing. As long as general objectives are the rule, our goals may
appear worthwhile to external observers. But once we start to describe
precisely what kinds of changes we are bringing about in the learner,
there is the danger that the public will reject our intentions as unworthy.
Yet, if what we are doing is trivial, educators should know it, and those
who support the educational institution should also know it. To the extent
that we are achieving innocuous behavior changes in learners, we are
guilty. We must abandon the ploy of "obfuscation by generality" and
make clear exactly what we are doing. Then we are obligated to defend
our choices.

Reason nine: Measurability implies accountability; teachers might
be judged on their ability to produce results in learners rather than on
the many bases now used as indices of competence.

This is a particularly threatening reason and serves to produce much
teacher resistance to precisely stated objectives. It doesn't take too much

insight on the part of the teacher to realize that if objectives are specified in terms of measurable learner behavior, there exists the possibility that the instructor will have to become *accountable* for securing such behavior changes. Teachers might actually be judged on their ability to bring about desirable changes in learners. They should be.

But a teacher should not be judged on the particular instructional *means* he uses to bring about desirable *ends.* At present many teachers are judged adversely simply because the instructional procedures they use do not coincide with those once used by an evaluator when "he was a teacher." In other words, if I'm a supervisor who has had considerable success with open-ended discussion, I may tend to view with disfavor any teachers who cleave to more directive methods. Yet, if the teacher using the more direct methods can secure learner behavior changes which are desirable, I have no right to judge that teacher as inadequate. The possibility of assessing instructional competence in terms of the teacher's ability to bring about specified behavior changes in learners brings with it far more assets than liabilities to the teacher. He will no longer be judged on the idiosyncratic whims of a visiting supervisor. Rather, he can amass evidence that, in terms of his pupils' actual attainments, he is able to teach efficiently.

Even though this is a striking departure from the current state of affairs, and a departure that may be threatening to the less competent, the educator must promote this kind of accountability rather than the maze of folklore and mysticism which exists at the moment regarding teacher evaluation.

Reason ten: It is far more difficult to generate such precise objectives than to talk about objectives in our customarily vague terms.

Here is a very significant objection to the development of precise goals. Teachers are, for the most part, far too busy to spend the necessary hours in stating their objectives and measurement procedures with the kind of precision implied by this discussion. It is said that we are soon nearing a time when we will have more teachers than jobs. This is the time to reduce the teacher's load to the point where he can become a professional decision-maker rather than a custodian. We must reduce public school teaching loads to those of college professors. This is the time when we must give the teacher immense help in specifying his objectives. Perhaps we should *give* him objectives from which to choose, rather than force him to generate his own. Many of the federal dollars currently being used to support education would be better spent on agencies which would produce alternative behavioral objectives for all fields at all grade levels. At any rate, the difficulty of the task should not preclude its accomplishment. We can recognize how hard the job is and still allocate the necessary resources to do it.

While these ten excuses are not exhaustive, they should suggest the nature of the reasons used to resist the implementation of precise instructional objectives. In spite of the very favorable overall reaction to explicit objectives during the past five to ten years, a small collection of dissident educators has arisen to oppose the quest for goal specificity. The trouble with criticisms of precise objectives isn't that they are completely without foundation. In fact, there are probably elements of truth in all of them. Yet, when we are attempting to promote the wide-scale adoption of precision in the classroom, there is the danger that many teachers will use the comments and objections of these few critics as an excuse for not thinking clearly about their goals. Any risks we run by moving to behavioral goals are miniscule in contrast with our current state of confusion regarding instructional intentions. Threatening or not, instructors must abandon their customary practices of goal-stating and turn to a framework of precision.

References

ARNSTINE, D. G. "The Language and Values of Programmed Instruction: Part 2." *The Educational Forum* 28 (1964), pp. 337–45.

BAKER, E. L., "The Differential Effect of Behavioral and Nonbehavioral Objectives Given to Teachers on the Achievements of Their Students" (Interim Report). (Washington, D.C.: U.S. Department of Health, Education, and Welfare, 1967.)

JACKSON, P. W., *The Way Teaching Is* (Washington, D.C.: Association for Supervision and Curriculum Development, N.E.A., 1966.)

KOMISAR, P. B., and J. E. MCCLELLAN, "Professor Arnstine and Programmed Instruction." Reprinted from *Educational Forum,* 1965.

MORSH, J. E., and E. WILDER, "Identifying the Effective Instructor: A Review of the Quantitative Studies, 1900–1952." U.S. Air Force Personnel Training Research Center, Research Bulletin No. AFPTRC-TR 54–44, 1954.

MUNRO, T., "The Interrelation of the Arts in Secondary Education." In *The Creative Arts in American Education* (Cambridge, Mass.: Harvard University Press, 1960).

POPHAM, W. J., "Development of a Performance Test of Teaching Proficiency" (Final Report). (Washington, D.C., U.S. Department of Health, Education, and Welfare, 1967.)

POPHAM, W. J., and E. L. BAKER, "Development of Performance Test of Teaching Proficiency." Paper presented at the annual meeting of the American Educational Research Association, New York, February, 1966.

PART THREE

Objectives-Oriented Educational Management Systems

In the past few years educational administrators have attempted to test the appropriateness of using measurable objectives in managing their operations. The initial selection in this section describes an effort by a network of innovative schools to organize their instructional endeavors around explicit goal statements. The second essay considers the application of measurable objectives to major educational systems such as large district or statewide operations. The final selection was based on a 1972 address at the National Association of Secondary School Principals in which an effort was made to alert school administrators to the uses of instructional objectives in today's quest for educational accountability.

7

Focus on Outcomes – A Guiding Theme of ES '70 Schools

ES '70 Schools are a group of secondary schools located in various parts of the United States. The name comes from the title of an ambitious, future-oriented program organized by the U.S. Office of Education called Educational Systems for the '70s. The purpose of the program was to exchange ideas for designing improved educational systems. Like so many comparable projects, the program failed to receive the continuing funding originally planned for it.

The single most important deficiency in American education is its preoccupation with instructional process. This overriding concern with procedures rather than the results produced by those procedures manifests itself in myriad ways. We see teachers judged according to the methods they use ("She has excellent chalkboard techniques and fine bulletin boards"). Innovation is lauded for its own sake ("Now there's a *really* new instructional approach!"). Teachers design classroom instructional sequences by asking themselves "What shall I do?" rather than the appropriate question, which is "What do I wish my learners to become?" Schools in the ES '70 network, fortunately, do not suffer from this debilitating affliction. Perhaps their example will stimulate other American educators to attend to more fruitful instructional concerns. Perhaps by their example they can promote a focus on outcomes. Only such a focus can remedy the educational ills fostered by process preoccupation.

A Means Orientation

Before turning to the schemes used by ES '70 schools in counteracting the devotees of process, a closer look at the culprits is in order. Essentially, the distinction is between educators who possess a means orientation and those who possess an outcomes orientation. Those who are captivated by questions of instructional process may well be descendants of the educational methods enthusiasts so prevalent during the early half of this century. More likely, they bear no such lineage—it's just a great deal easier to be concerned with instructional methods rather than with whether those methods are effective. For when you commit yourself to assessing whether a given instructional process is worthwhile, there are two frightfully aversive concomitants. First, you have to go to the very considerable trouble of devising adequate criterion measures. Second, you run the risk that you may be held accountable for producing satisfactory results.

Anyone who has seriously tried to develop criterion measures with which to assess a major instructional program will readily attest to the difficulty of such an enterprise. Simple, low-level objectives, of course, are easily assessed. All educators, or so it seems, are skilled in testing a student's ability to memorize. But assessing high-level cognitive outcomes or attitudinal attainments—this is a taxing task. The really worthwhile goals of education are invariably the most difficult to measure. Preparing adequate devices to assess such goals is onerous indeed.

Further, the accountability for instructional growth that is absent in means-oriented education is awesome, particularly for the incompetent. If one's responsibility ceases with the generation of instructional procedures, then there is no fear. The merits of the procedures will not be measured. One simply conjures up new ways of teaching people, then forgets it—or at most collects some impressionistic data from biased participants. Did the "experimental" teachers really like the new instructional method (with which they are clearly identified? How did the "experimental" pupils respond to the new approach? Having summarized such reactions, the means-oriented educator moves off to explore new instructional galaxies. The just-completed project has been a success.

But despite these two aversive elements, an outcomes-oriented approach to education is the only defensible stance open to the responsible educator. ES '70 educators have committed themselves to such an orientation. Let's examine the ingredients of such a commitment.

An Outcomes Orientation

An educator who focuses on outcomes, not process, is usually committed to the belief that teachers exist primarily to modify learners. More generally, formal education is viewed as an enterprise which is designed to *change* human beings so that they are better, wiser, more efficient, etc. If this basic assumption is correct (alternative assumptions appearing eminently untenable), then the educator's principal tasks are to (1) identify the kinds of modifications he wishes to promote, (2) design instructional procedures which he hopes will promote them, and (3) find out whether the procedures were successful. Judgments about the success of an instructional procedure are made exclusively on the basis of results, that is, the changes in learner behavior which emerge as a consequence of instruction. Only if the hoped-for changes in learner behavior have been attained is the instructional process considered effective. Only when such changes have not been attained is the process judged ineffective.

This concern with results, as reflected in the modified performance of learners, leads the outcomes-oriented educator to focus the bulk of his attention on the formulation of instructional objectives and, subsequently, on measuring the degree to which they have been achieved. Because the criterion by which the success of an instructional process will be judged must be measurable learner behavior, the outcomes-oriented educator cleaves exclusively to objectives amenable to measurement. Whether they are called "performance objectives," "behavioral goals," "operational objectives," or some equivalent phrase, they must be capable of post-instructional assessment.

But is the outcomes-oriented educator oblivious of instructional process? Clearly not. However, only *after* an appraisal of outcomes are modifications in procedures recommended. In other words, means are judged according to the ends achieved. Modifications of instructional means are often made, but only as dictated by the learner's post-instruction behavior.

ES '70 Schools

As pointed out earlier, the 19 ES '70 schools have committed themselves, in diverse ways, to an outcomes orientation. An examination of the several schemes by which these schools are employing measurably stated instructional objectives will illustrate the nature of this commitment.

Several of the schools are really just getting under way with respect to the employment of performance objectives. But at the very least, all network schools have provided specific training experiences, e.g., institutes, workshops, short courses, etc., to make their professional staffs more conversant with the manner in which instructional objectives can be most profitably formulated.

A few of the schools have engaged in what might be characterized as a generalized task analysis of the levels of specificity at which objectives should be stated. Two of the schools, for example, report attempts to explicate different levels of instructional objectives. The Breathitt County, Kentucky, ES '70 school has attempted to organize its instructional objectives at five levels of generality ranging from what are called "ultimate behavioral objectives" through the increasingly specific goals statements that follow, i.e., "terminal behavioral objective," "terminal intermediate behavioral objective," "intermediate behavioral objective," and "sub-behavioral objective." The Bloomfield Hills, Michigan, school district organizes instructional objectives into the following categories: "system objectives, discipline objectives, terminal performance objectives, interim performance objectives, and course objectives." While these attempts to classify instructional objectives have not yet been validated by experimental investigations, they illustrate considerable concern about the nature of instructional outcomes in these schools.

Several of the ES '70 schools have shown remarkable progress in developing instructional materials and evaluation measures based upon performance objectives. The accomplishments of Nova High School in Broward County, Florida, have been reported frequently during the past few years. This ES '70 school has developed small instructional units designated as Learning Activity Packages (LAPs) in science, mathematics, social studies, and technical science. These materials are used extensively in the school and, because of a liberal distribution policy, by a number of other secondary schools which have secured copies of the Nova LAPs. Development of additional learning activity packages in the areas of music, English, physical education, and language arts are now under way at Nova. The Monroe, Michigan, ES '70 school has also developed learning activity packages in metal shop, physics, and applied science. Monroe High School staff members have been willing to prepare these materials in addition to their regular instructional responsibilities. Some of the ES '70 schools have been able to provide more released time for these kinds of developmental activities than other network schools. The Philadelphia, Pennsylvania, school district has had a writing team working on the development of interdisciplinary instructional materials based on performance objectives for a number of months, even though their ES '70 school will not open until September, 1970.

In Duluth, Minnesota, the ES '70 high school has been using performance objectives in a highly individualized instructional program which, like the innovations at Nova, has been reported widely in recent years. One of the principal techniques for using measurable instructional objectives in Duluth is the development of student learning contracts. The key to the student learning contract is the performance objective. Students are provided with contracts in a variety of fields, each contract specifying the general purpose as well as the specific, measurable objective of the instructional activity. Sample test situations for the instructional objectives are provided along with resource materials which the student is to use in an attempt to achieve the instructional objective. The student than takes a test which measures attainment of the objective. If the student achieves the stated level of proficiency on the test, he is permitted to go on to another contract. If he fails to achieve the desired level, other instructional procedures (frequently a teacher-led presentation) help him to achieve the objective. A second test of equal difficulty is given to the student before he moves on to the next contract.

The ES '70 school in Mineola, New York, reports an unexpected dividend from focusing on measurable objectives. Eliot G. Spack, ES '70 coordinator in Mineola, described this incident as follows:

> Quite recently one of our elementary schools began to undertake a revision of its curriculum through the development of behavioral objectives in certain subject areas. At the time there was great concern registered by the teachers as to whether or not the central office would financially underwrite all the equipment and materials which they felt would be necessary for any individualized program. This group worked for several months under the guidance of the school principal. After almost a year of writing objectives and performance criteria the teachers were ready to review the array of resources which would be incorporated into the learning activities. The principal invited eight representatives of leading software producers to display their wares at a conference day session. The materials available reflected a potential expenditure in the thousands of dollars. Using their pre-defined objectives as their guide, the teachers surveyed the "market." When their review was completed the principal dismissed the salesmen and, mopping his brow in expectation of the worst, queried his staff on their desires. The sum total of their requests for purchase came to $12.60. The teachers had learned to become sophisticated consumers by applying their own objectives. It was quite a lesson for all!

As these varied uses of measurable objectives illustrate, there are certainly many procedures for employing specific outcomes in instructional planning and evaluation. But although the procedures were different, the central focus persisted, namely, that high quality instructional planning requires the explication of instructional intents in terms of measurable learner behaviors.

Reclassifying Outcomes

As the number of outcomes-oriented educators increases, the possibility of restructuring the basic curriculum patterns of American education also increases. Whereas the organization of curriculum according to classical subject and grade level boundaries is a time-honored tradition, there may be more functional ways to categorize instructional outcomes. Two research projects are currently under way at Rutgers University and at the University of California at Los Angeles to test the adequacy of alternative methods of classifying instructional outcomes. It is apparent that if we can find a large enough number of school personnel who are willing to consider outcomes rather than standard discipline and grade level classifications, there may be some merit in rethinking the basic organizational pattern of the curriculum. To illustrate, a child may acquire certain analytic skills in one course which are precisely the same as the analytic skills acquired in another course. It may be more efficient to organize the curriculum around that particular outcome, namely, that particular kind of analytic skill, than around the customary subject boundaries. The Rutgers and UCLA project staffs will be working closely with ES '70 schools to test both the adequacy of alternative methods of classifying instructional outcomes as well as the practical utility of such classification schemes in the public school classroom.

The major advantage of an outcomes-oriented approach to education is that our instructional outcomes have an increased probability of being realized. The major danger of such an approach is that we may be pursuing the wrong outcomes. Efforts to scrutinize methods of categorizing objectives, coupled with the highly visible outcomes orientation of the ES '70 network, offer the promise of both identifying and accomplishing truly worthwhile educational achievements.

8

Objectives-Based Management Strategies for Large Educational Systems

There is an apparent defect in human nature which disinclines us to subject any enterprise to careful scrutiny until we sense it is in some way defective. Without debating whether this failing stems from original sin or is merely an acquired shortcoming, there is little doubt that we are currently witnessing the results of this tendency in the field of education.

American citizens in increasing numbers have become disenchanted with the quality of our educational system, and the magnitude of this disenchantment has now passed the critical point, so that rhetoric no longer satisfies and corrective action is being demanded. The problem facing us now is easier to articulate than to answer, namely, "How should we go about promoting improvements in the educational enterprise?"

Systems Analysis Strategies

Some educators are turning to systems-analysis methodology as a possible source for satisfactory answers to this perplexing question. For certain of these systems-analysis proponents, one senses an almost religious devotion to their methodology, a devotion in which the litany of input analysis, output analysis, and servoloop feedback must be chanted daily—or at least in every published article and speech.

For me, however, systems-analysis approaches derive their merits not because they border on the occult but, rather, because they reflect a rational attempt to illuminate the areas in which we must make educational decisions. If most people are left to their own devices when they must make decisions, they will usually find that erroneous perceptions of reality and unconscious biases render those decisions less than satisfactory. Surely there are many wise human beings who will reach enlight-

This article is based on a presentation made at the annual meeting of the American Education Research Association, Chicago, April, 1972.

ened decisions that all of us would applaud, but there are many others who do not operate as meritoriously. If the decisions affect only themselves, we are not all that upset if the wrong choice is made. After all, an individual pretty well has the right to muck up his own life if he wishes. But in the field of education we see that imprudent decisions can penalize thousands of students, and thus we cannot remain as sanguine regarding intuitively based decision-making. Therefore, we find an increasing number of people, both educators and noneducators, advocating the use of more formal mechanisms for making decisions regarding large-scale enterprises. Customarily, these mechanisms have taken a form which more or less resembles a systems-analysis approach.

The distinguishing feature of a systems-analysis strategy is implied by its name. Clearly, there is an attempt to analyze a system of some sort, in this instance an educational system. But equally critical is the implication that this analysis will be a *systematic* one. Indeed, many people are enamoured of systems analysis approaches for precisely that reason— that is, they tend to reduce the capricious decision making which is so characteristic of most human endeavors.

There is another dimension characteristically associated with systems-analysis approaches that should be noticed, namely, a reliance on *evidence* of the system's effects. This orientation is in contrast to alternative approaches which, although systematic and analytic, are not essentially empirical methodologies. For instance, analytic philosophical approaches are generally not considered to be systems-analysis strategies even though they may epitomize rigorous analysis.

Large-Scale Educational Systems

This discussion will be restricted to the consideration of large-scale educational enterprises, such as a state school system or a large school district. For example, California legislators are undertaking a serious appraisal of the state's master plan for higher education. One of the considerations of the planners relates to the development of an evaluation system that will permit the state legislators and other concerned citizens within the state to judge the quality of the California higher education system.

This does not suggest that the following observations are inappropriate for small systems, such as a moderate-sized school district or even a single school. Yet, in general, the focus will be on the recommendations for systems of sufficient magnitude to warrant the considerable investment in carrying out the procedures that will be described.

Objectives-Based Systems Analysis

In most systems-analysis models there are three sets of questions to be answered. These questions are associated with the three major phases of managing a system (see Figure 1). There are questions regarding which *inputs* should be made to the system, that is, the purposes for which the system exists and the types of resources that will be used to attain those purposes. A second set of questions is associated with the actual *operation* of the system—that is, how well are things working? A final group of questions stems from an appraisal of the *output* of the system—that is, was the effectiveness of the system such that it should remain essentially unmodified or do we have to make some changes in it?

Now there is nothing inherent in systems-analysis models that requires us to employ instructional objectives as an organizing rubric in the implementation of a model. There may be preferable classification schemes for organizing the data that must be processed in a systems-analysis scheme. However, we are presently addressing ourselves to a systems-analysis strategy in which instructional objectives play a prominent role. The choice to employ objectives as the organizing dimension stems from a belief that statements of instructional objectives can serve as parsimonious vehicles for communicating the information that must be considered at various points in analyzing the system. Note, for instance, that those individuals operating the National Assessment of Educational Progress, surely dealing with a large-scale educational enterprise, have chosen to employ statements of instructional objectives as their organizing rubric.

For example, a learner's status in connection with an educational system may be represented by his or her performance on an examination of some sort. Rather than requiring a decision maker to scrutinize the entire examination, we may convey an idea of what the examination entails by identifying the learner competencies it was designed to measure. Often these competencies can be described as a *desired* status for the learner, hence the equivalent of an instructional objective. In addition, many educators are quite familiar with the general concept of instructional objectives, this topic having received ample attention during the past decade.

To reiterate, it is not requisite to employ instructional objectives as the organizing theme for an educational systems-analysis model.

FIGURE 1. A Simplified System Model.

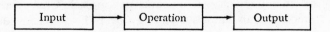

Nonetheless, the use of objectives for this purpose seems to offer some advantages and, accordingly, the remaining paragraphs will be used to describe a systems-analysis model for large educational enterprises that prominently employs instructional objectives.

Measurable Objectives

It is important to note at the outset of this discussion that, unless otherwise noted, we will use the term "instructional objective" to represent a *measurable* instructional objective. Because measurable objectives communicate our instructional intentions with less ambiguity than broad, general objectives, it would seem particularly important to use such objectives in a rational decision-making scheme where any extra system noise (such as ambiguous symbology) will reduce the quality of the decisions. In recent years, of course, there have been numerous treatises written regarding technical questions of how such measurable objectives should be optimally formulated.

Returning now to the general questions that an educational systems analyst must attempt to answer, we can turn first to what is perhaps the most important question facing any systems designer. This question is, "To what ends should the system be committed?" Putting it another way, "Why should the education system be there in the first place?" For an objectives for a large-scale educational system, and these are somewhat problem of goal determination.

Goal Determination

In general, the proponent of systems analysis approaches subscribes to a classic means/ends paradigm. It is anticipated that if proper ends can be identified it will be worth the trouble to test the efficacy of alternative means to achieve those ends until certain means can be identified which do the job. In the field of education we are becoming increasingly more sophisticated in designing instructional sequences. It thus becomes increasingly imperative to identify the most defensible goals of our educational systems so that improved instructional means can be directed toward the proper ends.

There are at least two approaches to specifying the appropriate objectives for a large-scale educational system, and these are somewhat analogous to an inductive versus a deductive approach. Characteristically, we have employed an inductive strategy over the years in education.

According to this scheme the educational planner consults various groups with a series of general questions, such as "What do you want our schools to accomplish?" People typically respond to such questions with varying degrees of specificity, so it is usually up to the educational planner to synthesize their somewhat diffuse reactions and translate them into more or less definitive goal statements. Ralph Tyler's curriculum model, which has, at least at a theoretical level, been quite influential during the past several decades, represents such an approach.

An alternative attack on the goal-determination problem has become available in recent years through the establishment of large pools of measurable instructional objectives. Various clienteles can rate objectives from these pools as to the appropriateness of their inclusion in the curriculum of a given education system. In this latter approach, therefore, we do not try to derive statements of objectives from the value preferences and informal assertions of people; rather, we present people with objectives from which they choose those they consider most important.

Perhaps because the latter approach seems to offer a greater possibility of systematization through technical refinement, it has received more attention. Particularly as a consequence of the *needs-assessment* operations required by federal ESEA Title III funding programs, we find more and more educators who are attempting to rigorously establish objectives for large-scale educational endeavors. A number of these efforts have involved the use of deductively designated educational objectives.

The general strategy in an objectives-based goal-determination operation involves presentation of alternative sets of educational objectives to groups who have a stake in deciding what the goals of the system ought to be. These groups then rate, rank, or in other ways display their preferences regarding those objectives. The expressed preferences of the various groups are then surveyed by those who must ultimately decide on the systems' goals and, hopefully, more enlightened judgments regarding what the system's goals ought to be can be made on the basis of such preference data.

The somewhat new feature of this approach to goal determination involves the use of measurable objectives. In previous efforts to employ this general strategy educators often used loose, nonmeasurable goals which almost served as Rorschach ink blots for those expressing their preferences—that is to say, people read into nebulous goal statements almost anything they wished. As a consequence, it was extremely difficult to make reasonable contrasts among the preferences of various groups. With the use of measurable objectives, fortunately, ambiguity is reduced, and as a consequence differences among various clienteles are more directly a function of their real differences in values rather than confusion regarding the meaning of certain goal statements.

The kinds of groups that might be involved, of course, will vary from one educational enterprise to another. For instance, in the California higher education evaluation system it would seem imperative to involve student groups from the various types of higher education institutions within the state, namely, community colleges, state colleges, and universities. It would seem equally important to involve citizen groups of various kinds, such as parents, businessmen, and other public-spirited citizens. This would be an ideal opportunity, for example, to secure preference inputs from ethnic groups and other minorities who often feel that large educational systems are unresponsive to their particular curricular preferences. It might be particularly appropriate to secure the reactions of a group of specially designated *futurists* whose charge would be to consider higher education objectives in light of their suitability for the 1980's and 1990's, not merely for the next few years. The preferences of these groups can be coalesced and represented in straightforward numerical form in any one of several methods.[1]

To illustrate an alternative, somewhat less quantitative method of establishing priorities among competing objectives, Professor Robert E. Stake of the University of Illinois has recently devised an approach to priorities planning in which the decision makers consider such data as the preferences of various clienteles. However, they also survey the system's requisite resource allocations, the payoff probabilities of various objectives, and the relevant contingency conditions—that is, circumstances that call for change in instructional procedures.[2]

Having established the preferred objectives of a system, an important second step in the goal determination is to discover the degree to which the target learners can already display the hoped-for behaviors designated by the various reference groups. This is where measurable instructional objectives offer considerable advantages, for since the objectives that have been rated by the various groups are stated in explicit and measurable terms, it is a relatively straightforward task to devise measuring devices from those objectives and, as a consequence, to measure the learner's status.

Now we would certainly employ item and person sampling techniques in this approach in order to conserve testing time and to make the task economically feasible. But by using such techniques, whereby only certain students are sampled and those sampled completed only segments of the total measuring devices, we can certainly measure student attainment of the high-priority goals established with the previous rating/ranking procedure.

The next step, then, is to contrast the learner's status with the high-priority goals and decide which of these we wish to direct our educational enterprise toward. Clearly, there are still a great many value judgments to be made at this point, but the hope is that by making the decisions as heavily data-based as possible, superior decisions will be made.

This system of goal determination by having different clienteles rate extant objectives has been tried out for the past two years by the Instructional Objectives Exchange (IOX) with some interesting results.[3] Working with several school districts in Southern California, IOX has secured a number of ratings of different objectives within the IOX collections by students, teachers, parents, and futurists. Various modifications in the directions to the rater groups have yielded some insights regarding the suitability of such matters as the inclusion of sample measurement items to further clarify the meaning of the objective, the use of rankings versus ratings, and so forth. Perhaps the most important conclusion drawn from these studies relates to the number of objectives to be rated. It now appears to the IOX staff, in contrast to earlier expectations, that it is simply unwise to present a vast array of instructional objectives to rater groups. In other words, even though in certain of the collections of objectives currently distributed by the Instructional Objectives Exchange there are upwards of one or two hundred objectives, it makes little sense to attempt to secure ratings of so many objectives. Frankly, the educational decision maker is generally not able to process the resulting data from such rating analyses. Instead, the conclusion from the IOX work to date suggests that it would be far better to present a more moderate number of *content general* objectives, that is, measurable objectives that describe a *class* of learner behaviors rather than a single series of specific test items, and have these more general objectives rated by appropriate groups.

This is a particularly difficult procedure because one of the more persistent problems having to do with the technology of objectives concerns the *level of generality* of those objectives. Individuals working with instructional objectives since Ralph Tyler's early efforts have pointed out that the level-of-specificity question or, conversely, the level-of-generality issue, is one of the most important questions needing to be resolved in the field of instructional objectives. Yet no one seems to have come up with a very satisfactory solution. Our general estimate at this point, however, is that we must find some way to present larger "chunks" of educational objectives to various groups for ratings. Ending up with more than twenty-five or thirty objectives that must be rated, is, to most humans, an unmanageable intellectual task.

It is interesting to note that in certain relatively large school districts in the state of California the number of reading objectives has been reduced to only three or four, thus a single objective—for instance, a student's ability to decode twenty-five words randomly drawn from a list of 500—serves to represent the bulk of that district's reading effort.

It is quite apparent that more attention must be given to the matter of how general an objective should be in order for it to prove serviceable in this type of situation. At one extreme, however, the experience at IOX to date suggests that far fewer objectives be employed than we have characteristically been using.

Progress Monitoring

The second set of questions of concern to those involved in decisions regarding educational systems concerns the appraisal of the progress of the system toward its stipulated goals. One relatively straightforward method of discerning the degree to which the system's goals are being accomplished involves the administration of criterion-referenced tests associated with the various system goals so that indications of learner progress toward those goals can be secured. Goals which, according to measured learner progress, are not being achieved can be attacked with alternative instructional strategies, additional resources, and so on. Goals that are being achieved on schedule permit the inference that the instructional program is working as well as needed. It is even conceivable, of course, that some goals will be achieved ahead of schedule, thereby permitting a shifting of resources toward less effective instructional activities.

It is particularly important in assessing progress toward system goals to gather the requisite data as economically as possible. Once more, matrix sampling (a technical term for item sampling combined with person sampling) is a valuable ally of the educational evaluator. It is even possible, when resources are short, to combine matrix sampling with goal sampling by using a technique whereby progress toward only certain goals is monitored. Such an approach, of course, does not give information about all of the system's goals, hence, it suffers from the defect of supplying only partial information. Nonetheless, where a system simply does not have the financial resources to investigate satisfactorily the progress toward all goals, the use of goal sampling may represent a reasonable alternative.

It is at this juncture that the evaluator should be particularly attentive to unanticipated consequences of the educational system's operation. Whereas educational designers can spell out carefully the hoped-for outcomes of an educational enterprise, it is often the case that some unintended and aversive consequences ensue which were simply unforeseen by the instructional designers. Michael Scriven argues cogently for the use of goal-free evaluation in which the educational evaluator is attentive to the consequences of an educational system, not to the rhetoric of the instructional designers. Scriven suggests that under certain circumstances it may be more judicious to examine what happens as a consequence of the program rather than what the instructional designers say will occur through the use of their stated objectives. Whether one uses goal-free-evaluation approaches or simply employs considerable circumspection regarding what might have gone wrong, it is quite important to attend to all of the effects of a program, not only those which were intended.

Output Appraisal

The final set of questions regarding the management of a large-scale educational system concerns the final quality of its results. Once more, since we are using objectives as an organizing rubric, it is possible to develop criterion-referenced tests that are congruent with those objectives and administer them on a matrix-sampling basis to the learners served by the system. Results on such measures, combined with measures of unanticipated consequences akin to those described in the previous paragraph, will yield the kind of evidence necessary to reach a judgment regarding the quality of the educational enterprise.

A particularly thorny problem arises related to the manner in which results of such an analysis should be reported. Educational evaluators are only now beginning to wrestle seriously with alternative vehicles for reporting evaluative results in such a way that decision makers can take appropriate action based on the evaluation data. All too frequently we find evaluation endeavors resulting in encyclopedic final reports that only a person of great devotion has the patience to read completely. Brevity is a desirable criterion in reporting results of evaluation studies irrespective of the type of evaluation report involved.

Again, the organizing theme for evaluation, at least for the approach being described here, would be the use of instructional objectives. Progress toward the major instructional objectives adopted by the educational system would be reported to the appropriate decision-making groups, such as local school boards, state school boards, or university regents. In a general before-after model it is important to present the data in as succinct a fashion as possible so that those utilizing the results can make more sense out of them. Here is where the educational evaluator will have to be particularly judicious in the data he selects to report and the manner in which those data are described.

Theory and Practice

In the foregoing paragraphs a general strategy for the management of large educational enterprises has been described. Clearly, the discussion has been at a very general, not on a nuts-and-bolts level. Sometimes one has the feeling that in propounding a given theoretical point of view an effort to implement it in practice will result in chaos. The technical problems are seen as too serious to work out.

For example, I often hear an aptitude x treatment interaction specialist suggest that if we could only sort out pupils' learning styles and judiciously mesh them with relevant instructional treatments, then educational Valhalla would be upon us. At a theoretical level I can applaud such a stance, but in my pragmatic heart of hearts I really doubt that this can be pulled off, at least in my lifetime. The practical problems are too sticky.

With present propositions, however, this does not seem to be the case. Surely there will be technical, procedural questions that must be dealt with. For example, exactly which groups will be involved in rating the objectives that will result in the selection of goals for the system? How many learners should be tested in order to yield reasonable estimates regarding the progress of the system as well as its final output? What kinds of departures from anticipated progress should dictate modifications in the system? These and other problems can be faced and, I believe, resolved by individuals wishing to seriously monitor the progress of a large-scale educational enterprise.

But that kind of operation takes more money than most educators have been willing to spend. Other than the recently initiated Experimental Schools Program of the U.S. Office of Education we see few large-scale educational enterprises in which ample funds have been set aside for evaluation. Most state and local school systems operate under an explicit evaluation budget of less than 1 percent, if that much. The kind of evaluation endeavor we're talking about here clearly will demand resources of around 5 percent or better. The first-blush reluctance of individuals to spend that kind of money should be countered by hard-nosed estimates of the benefits, both economic and educational, that can be derived from rigorously evaluating the progress of a large-scale educational undertaking.

Perfection and Imperfectability

Some detractors will allege quite accurately that systems approaches such as those described here are laden with flaws. Surely by using objectives-based systems we will discover that certain critical features of the educational system are not appraised with sufficient sensitivity to yield the right kind of information for making proper decisions. When faced with these kinds of criticisms, however, I am reminded that decisions must currently be made regarding educational enterprises, day in and day out. And at the moment these decisions are being made with far less sophistication, far less data, and far less accuracy than might be rendered under a system such as that proposed herein. Granted that a systems-analysis approach is not perfect, it nevertheless seems to offer a clear improvement over the general quality of decision making seen so prevalently these days in educational arenas. And, perhaps more importantly, because of its systematic nature such an approach is amenable to technical self-correction and, eventually, incremental improvement so that even if the management system lacks total perfection, it will be so close that the learners it serves won't know the difference.

References

1. See, for example, "Determining Defensible Goals via Educational Needs Assessment" (Los Angeles: Vimcet Associates, P.O. Box 24714, 1971).
2. STAKE, ROBERT E. *Priorities Planning: Judging the Importance of Alternative Objectives* (Los Angeles: Instructional Objectives Exchange, 1972).
3. POPHAM, W. JAMES, *Providing Wide Ranging, Diversely Organized Pools of Instructional Objectives and Measures,* Final Report for the U.S. Office of Education (Project 14-0563, Grant OEG-0-9-140563-4635-085), Department of Health, Education, and Welfare, 1971.

9

The New World of
Accountability: In the Classroom

The educational battle lines for the impending accountability show-down are drawn as clearly as in a classic western movie. On one side we have the underdog public school teachers, their portable classrooms drawn into a circle. On the other side is the marauding Accountability Gang who, although they are viewed by teachers as mortal enemies, could hardly be considered *no-account* bandits. The Accountability Gang is beginning to fire some pretty potent pistols at the embattled teachers. For instead of Colt six-shooters and Winchester rifles, their guns bear different markings. One is labeled "Teacher Tenure." Another is called "Teacher Evaluation." A third simply says "Taxpayer's Revolt." It is small wonder that bullets from these guns may pick off a teacher or two. And the terrifying part of this script, at least to classroom teachers, is that there may be no cavalry over the next hill coming to the rescue.

While perhaps a mite less melodramatic, the present real-world plight of classroom teachers who are seriously trying to cope with the educational-accountability movement is equally serious. Teachers are being quite literally bombarded with requests and/or directives to become more accountable for their instructional activities. Just what does this mean and how can a willing teacher react sensibly to the current quest for accountability?

Well, in general the concept of educational accountability involves the teacher's producing *evidence* regarding the quality of his or her teaching, usually in terms of what happens to pupils, then standing ready to be judged on the basis of that evidence. An accountable teacher, therefore, takes *responsibility* for the results his or her instruction produces in learners. Characteristically, other individuals, e.g., supervisors, administrators, or school board members, will then take appropriate action based

Reprinted from the May, 1972, *Bulletin of the National Association of Secondary School Principals*, Vol. 56, No. 364, p. 25.

on those results. The "appropriate action" might range from decisions regarding which courses the teacher should teach next year all the way to termination of services or salary increases and decreases. Clearly, the stakes are high.

Further, the situation has moved well beyond the empty rhetoric stage. California legislators last year [1971] enacted a teacher evaluation law requiring each K–12 teacher in the state to be evaluated (probationary teachers annually, all others biennially) by locally devised teacher-appraisal systems. These local evaluation systems must include certain *state-stipulated* elements. Prominent among these legislative required elements is the teacher's role in promoting *learner progress* in each area of study toward locally defined standards. Thus, a learner-results criterion has been mandated by California lawmakers for teacher evaluation. A state-wide system of imposed accountability therefore exists in California. Other states will surely be observing the implementation of the California teacher-evaluation law with keen interest.

Beyond their individual involvement in the accountability milieu as it affects job security and advancement, teachers are also being asked to play an integral role in the appraisal of larger educational units, e.g., the school or school district. The public is clearly subjecting educational institutions to increased scrutiny. Citizens are not elated with their perceptions of the quality of education. They want dramatic improvements in the schools and, unless they get them, there is real doubt as to whether we can expect much increased financial support for our educational endeavors. And the public is in no mood to be assuaged by promises. *"Deliver the results,"* we are being told. No longer will lofty language suffice, and yesteryear's assurances that "only we professionals know what we're doing" must seem laughable to today's informed layman.

The distressing fact is that we haven't produced very impressive results for the nation's children. There are too many future voters who can't read satisfactorily, can't reason respectably, don't care for learning in general, and are pretty well alienated from the larger adult society.

Well, what do educators do about this demand that they produce results? How should they respond to the mounting pressure that they become more accountable? My recommendation is that we do just that— *we produce results and we become accountable!* For that stance, in my estimate, is the only professionally defensible posture available to us, and we should be chagrined that it took external forces to spur us to action.

Putting historical antecedents aside, let's seize the initiative in this drive to make educators responsible for their actions. The vast majority of American teachers are well-intentioned men and women who want only the best for the children under their tutelage. Impeded only by their human limitations. (there are only 24 hours available in most days, and most human folk can't psychologically work 18 of those), most teachers would like to do a better job for their pupils if they only knew how. And here's where the school principal comes in—his role should be to increase the teacher's skill in achieving *demonstrable* results with learners, while at the same time making sure those results are the most defensible ones that can be attained.

In brief, I am suggesting that we accept the accountability challenge by increasing classroom teachers' skills in producing evidence that their instruction yields worthwhile results for learners. Not only is this the key ingredient in current accountability strategies, it represents a way of helping teachers do the best job they can for their students.

Space limitations preclude an exhaustive analysis of the numerous ways we can offer succor to the classroom teacher in promoting their increased results-producing competence. Thus, I would like to outline only two such strategies, but two strategies which seem to me to be high payoff schemes for implementing the principal's leadership role in this endeavor.

Since the emphasis is on getting demonstrable results, we should get into the teacher's hands suitable measures of such results. The teacher can then more readily monitor the quality of instruction in relationship to student progress on such measures and, insofar as resources permit, make individual diagnoses and prescriptions for different learners on the basis of their performance on such measures. This is a stance totally compatible with the continuing emphasis on measurable instructional objectives seen so frequently in today's educational circles. But rather than forcing the already too busy teacher to conjure up a host of specific objectives and measures related to them, *we have to provide these measures.*

I believe that criterion-referenced measures related to objectives will prove serviceable merely because experience suggests that explicit objectives will be a more parsimonious way of describing a class of learner behaviors than by using the measuring device itself. And please note that by measuring device I do not mean only paper-and-pencil tests. Surely the bulk of these measures will, for practicality's sake, be in a paper format. But we can use paper-formatted measures for more diverse assessment schemes than the classic multiple-choice test. Attitudinal inventories, interest questionnaires, indeed, affective measures of all sorts, can be handled by low-cost, paper measuring devices.

But why use such criterion-referenced measures rather than the time-honored standardized tests? A simple question, with a simple answer. Because *for purposes of measuring results reflecting high-quality instruction, standardized tests are usually inappropriate.* They were designed, developed, and refined with a totally different purpose in mind, namely, to permit us to distinguish between different learners. For the purpose for which they were intended, standardized tests are fine. When selections among learners are in order, for instance, in predicting which students will succeed in college, standardized tests are super. Well, at least, until some of their ethnic biases are better eliminated, they're the best available. But for purposes of assessing the quality of instruction and for making specific judgments about what certain pupils have learned, standardized tests will typically yield misleading information.

We need more short-duration tests which have better *local curricular validity.* There are several ways school principals can attempt to promote the availability of more of these measures. First, they can bring concentrated pressure on America's major test publishers to encourage them to move more rapidly into the development of criterion-referenced measures. Second, they can inspect the suitability of those criterion-referenced measuring devices currently available. Third, if local resources permit, they can develop at least a few measures to deal with particularly high-priority goals (perhaps in concert with neighboring schools or school districts).

Once the measures are available, teachers should be encouraged to use them frequently and to make instructional modifications as dictated by the results. And for purposes of instructional evaluation, not every pupil needs to complete every measure in its entirety. The use of *item sampling,* whereby different pupils complete only a small segment of the measuring device, can yield accurate estimates of group performance while conserving valuable instructional time.

The whole thrust of this particular strategy is to provide measures of pupil outcomes so that teachers will not have to judge intuitively whether their instructional tactics are effective, for such intuitions are often as likely to be wrong as they are to be right. Decisions regarding whether to modify or retain a given instructional sequence can be better made by the classroom teacher on the basis of data yielded from criterion-referenced measures.

Instructional Mini-lessons

One vehicle which appears to offer considerable promise in helping classroom teachers increase their ability to produce desirable results with learners is the *instructional mini-lesson,* or sometimes called the *teaching*

performance test. By employing these mini-lessons in a systematic inservice or pre-service program there is evidence that instructors can increase
their teaching proficiency. For example, Martin Levine has found that
teachers who have attempted to improve their instructional effectiveness
through the use of mini-lessons have been able to significantly outperform
comparable teachers not participating in a mini-lesson improvement program. Further, teachers well versed in instructional principles and experienced with mini-lessons have been able to dramatically exceed the
performance of novice teachers. There is evidence beginning to build up
which, although only suggestive at the moment, offers considerable support for the role of mini-lessons in pre-service and in-service teacher
education programs.

In general, instructional mini-lessons are designed to improve a
teacher's skill in accomplishing a prespecified instructional objective while
at the same time promoting learner interest in the lesson. Here's how
they work:

> *First,* a teacher is given an explicit instructional objective along
> with a sample measurement item showing how the objective's
> achievement will be measured.
>
> *Second,* the teacher is given time to plan a lesson designed to
> achieve the objective.
>
> *Third,* the teacher instructs a group of learners for a specified
> period of time, perhaps as few as a half dozen students or as many
> as a whole class. Certain mini-lessons are designed to be used with
> adult learners, others with younger learners.
>
> *Fourth,* the learners are measured with a post-test based on the
> objective but unseen previously by the teacher. Learner interest in
> the instruction is also measured.

On the basis of these two indicators, that is, learners' interest ratings and
post-test scores, a judgment of the teacher's instructional skill can be
derived. Such a judgment does not reflect all dimensions on which a
teacher should be judged, only the teacher's ability to accomplish a prespecified instructional objective with positive learner affect during a
short lesson. Nevertheless, this is an important aspect of a teacher's
instructional proficiency.

The use of mini-lessons to bring about increases in a teacher's
instructional skill is consistent with a basic assumption regarding teaching, namely, that the chief reason for a teacher's existence in the classroom is to bring about desirable changes in learners. Accordingly, one
important competency which a teacher should possess is the ability to

promote the learner's attainment of specific instructional objectives. Mini-lessons are designed to assess this ability, that is, the teacher's skill in accomplishing pre-specified instructional objectives. Mini-lessons, therefore, can be used as the central focus of pre-service and in-service programs which set out to improve this key instructional skill. Unlike the increasingly popular micro-teaching procedures, the focus of instructional mini-lessons is on learner outcomes, not the procedures employed by the teacher, that is, mini-lessons are product-focused rather than process-focused.

Even though the two specific procedures described here clearly do not exhaust the range of potential approaches we might employ to aid classroom teachers in improving their ability to produce better results, they are certainly consistent with the general theme of increasing the degree to which a teacher should become accountable. If educators can only capitalize on the correct state of educational affairs, rather than being cast in the role of progress-resistors, we may mark the age of accountability as the beginning of a new era indeed.

PART FOUR
Extending Objectives Into Measurement and Evaluation

The impact of objectives-oriented approaches to instruction has extended well beyond the confines of curriculum and instruction. The first selection in this section, coauthored with the late T.R. Husek, deals with distinctions between norm-referenced and criterion-referenced approaches to measurement. We could have as easily described the latter as objectives-based rather than criterion-referenced, for that is essentially the kind of measurement strategy we had in mind. The second selection offers a procedure for evaluating instructional programs with some objectives in common and some that are dissimilar.

10

Implications of Criterion-Referenced Measurement

The question of what score to use as the most meaningful index of a
student's performance on a test has been the subject of many discussions
over the years. Percentile scores, raw scores, and standard scores of various kinds have been advocated. The arguments have almost always
begun with the premise that the test is a given and that the issue is how
to obtain the meaningful score. That is, there has been general acceptance
of how the test should be constructed and judged. Test theory as
explicated in most elementary testing texts has been assumed to represent
a commonly held set of values. In recent years some writers (for example,
Cronbach and Gleser, 1965) have begun to question the usefulness of
classical test theory for all testing problems. This broadens and compli-
cates the question above; the problem is now not only how to summarize
a student's performance on a test, but also how to insure that a test is
constructed (and judged) in a manner appropriate to its use, even if its
use is not in the classical framework.

One facet of this issue has particular relevance to tests based on
instructional objectives. For several years now, particularly since the
appearance of Glaser's article (1963) on the subject, measurement and
instructional specialists have been drawing distinctions between so-called
norm-referenced and *criterion-referenced* approaches to measurement.
But it appears that, other than adding new terms to the technical lexicon,
the two constructs have made little difference in measurement practice.
Perhaps the reason for this is that few analyses have been made of the
practical implications of using criterion-referenced measures. Most of us
are familiar with concepts associated with norm-referenced measurement.

This article was coauthored by T. R. Husek. Reprinted from the Spring, 1969, issue
of *Journal of Educational Measurement*, Vol. 8, No. 3. Copyright 1969 by the
National Council of Measurement in Education, East Lansing, Michigan.

We grew up with them. A criterion-referenced approach, however, is another matter. What differences, if any, does a criterion-referenced framework make with respect to such operations as test construction and revision, and to such concepts as reliability and validity? This article will examine some of these implications by contrasting criterion-referenced and norm-referenced approaches with respect to such central measurement notions.

It is not possible to tell a *norm-referenced* test from a *criterion-referenced* test by looking at it. In fact a *criterion-referenced* test could also be used as a *norm-referenced* test—although the reverse is not so easy to imagine. However, this truth should not be allowed to obscure the extremely important differences between these two approaches to testing.

At the most elementary level, norm-referenced measures are those which are used to ascertain an individual's performance in relationship to the performance of other individuals on the same measuring device. The meaningfulness of the individual score emerges from the comparison. It is because the individual is compared with some normative group that such measures are described as norm-referenced. Most standardized tests of achievement or intellectual ability can be classified as norm-referenced measures.

Criterion-referenced measures are those which are used to ascertain an individual's status with respect to some criterion, i.e., performance standard. It is because the individual is compared with some established criterion, rather than other individuals, that these measures are described as criterion-referenced. The meaningfulness of an individual score is not dependent on comparison with other testees. We want to know what the individual can do, not how he stands in comparison to others. For example, the dog owner who wants to keep his dog in the back yard may give his dog a fence-jumping test. The owner wants to find out how high the dog can jump so that the owner can build a fence high enough to keep the dog in the yard. How the dog compares with other dogs is irrelevant. Another example of a criterion-referenced test would be the Red Cross Senior Lifesaving Test, where an individual must display certain swimming skills to pass the examination irrespective of how well others perform on the test.

Since norm-referenced measures are devised to facilitate comparisons among individuals, it is not surprising that their primary purpose is to make decisions about *individuals*. Which pupil should be counseled to pursue higher education? Which pupils should be advised to attain vocational skills? These are the kinds of questions one seeks to answer through the use of norm-referenced measures, for many decisions regarding an individual can best be made by knowing more about the "competition," that is, by knowing how other, comparable individuals perform.

Criterion-referenced tests are devised to make decisions both about *individuals and treatments*, e.g., instructional programs. In the case of decisions regarding individuals, one might use a criterion-referenced test to determine whether a learner had mastered a criterion skill considered prerequisite to his commencing a new training program. In the case of decisions regarding treatments, one might design a criterion-referenced measure which reflected a set of instructional objectives supposedly achieved by a replicable instructional sequence. By administering the criterion-referenced measure to appropriate learners after they had completed the instructional sequence, one could reach a decision regarding the efficacy of the sequence (treatment).

Although both norm-referenced and criterion-referenced tests are used to make decisions about individuals, there is usually a difference in the two contexts in which such decisions are made. Generally, a norm-referenced measure is employed where a degree of *selectivity* is required by the situation. For example, when there are only limited openings in a company's executive training program, the company is anxious to identify the *best* potential trainees. It is critical in such situations, therefore, that the measure permit *relative* comparisons among individuals. On the other hand, in situations where one is only interested in whether an individual possesses a particular competence, and there are no constraints regarding how many individuals can possess that skill, criterion-referenced measures are suitable. Theoretically, at the close of many instructional programs we might hope that *all* learners would display *maximum* proficiency on measures reflecting the instructional objectives. In this sense, of course, criterion-referenced measures may be considered *absolute* indicators. Thus, both norm-referenced and criterion-referenced tests can be focused on decisions regarding individuals—it is the context within which these decisions are made that really produces the distinction.

Now one could, of course, use norm-referenced measures as well as criterion-referenced measures to make decisions regarding the merits of instructional programs. Certainly, this has been a common practice through the years as educators have evaluated their curriculum efforts on the basis of pupil performance on standardized examinations. But norm-referenced measures were really designed to "spread people out" and, as we shall see, are best suited to that purpose.

With this initial distinction in mind, we shall now examine the implications of the two approaches to measurement, particularly with respect to criterion-referenced measures, for these topics: variability, item construction, reliability, validity, item analysis, reporting and interpretation.

Variability

The issue of variability is at the core of the difference between norm-referenced and criterion-referenced tests. Since the meaningfulness of a norm-referenced score is basically dpendent on the relative position of the score in comparison with other scores, the more variability in the scores the better. With a norm-referenced test, we want to be able to tell Jamie from Joey from Frank, and we feel more secure about telling them apart if their scores are very different.

With criterion-referenced tests, variability is irrelevant. The meaning of the score is not dependent on comparison with other scores; it flows directly from the connection between the items and the criterion. It is, of course, true that one almost always gets variant scores on any psychological test; but that variability is not a necessary condition for a good criterion-referenced test.

The subtle and not-so-subtle implications of this central difference in the relevance of variability must permeate any discussion of the two approaches to testing. For example, we all have been told that a test should be reliable and valid. We have all read about test construction and item analysis. The procedures may not always be simple, the formulas may not be trivial; but there are hundreds of books and thousands of articles to guide us. Unfortunately, most of what these "helpmates" outline as "good" things to do are not only irrelevant to criterion-referenced tests, but are actually injurious to their proper development and use. This is true because the treatments of validity, the suggestions about reliability, and the formulas for item analysis are all based on the desirability of variability among scores. The connection may not be obvious but it is always there.

Item Construction

The basic difference between item construction in norm-referenced and criterion-referenced frameworks is a matter of "set" on the part of the item writer. Until we reach that automated era when computers can cough forth many items per minute, someone is going to have to construct them. The primary differences in purposes of norm-referenced and criterion-referenced measurement will usually influence the item writer to a considerable degree in at least one very significant way and, possibly to a lesser extent, in a second way as well.

Most important, when a writer constructs items for a norm-referenced test, he wants variability and, as a consequence, makes all sorts of concessions, sometimes subtle, sometimes obvious, to promote variant scores. He disdains items which are "too easy" or "too hard."

He tries to increase the allure of wrong-answer options. All of this he does to produce variability. Occasionally this overriding criterion may reduce the adequacy of the instrument, for even spurious factors may be incorporated in items just to produce variance.

The criterion-referenced item writer is guided by another goal. His chief rule is to make sure the item is an accurate reflection of the criterion behavior. Difficult or easy, discriminating or indiscriminate, the important thing is to make the item represent the class of behaviors delimited by the criterion. Those who write criterion-referenced items are usually far more attentive to defining the domain of relevant test responses and the situations in which they should be required. This rather fundamental difference in "set" on the part of criterion-referenced and norm-referenced item writers can clearly contribute to differences in the resulting items.

A second difference associated with test construction is that although norm-referenced and criterion-referenced measures which are used to make decisions regarding individuals require that the same test (or an equivalent form) be used with different individuals, criterion-referenced tests used for evaluating programs need not. The concept of item sampling (Cronbach, 1963; Husek and Sirotnik, 1968) in which different people complete different items (thereby permitting the sampling of more behavior with shorter tests) is highly appropriate for evaluating the adequacy of treatments. Thus, for such situations a number of different test forms, each containing different criterion-referenced items, could be constructed. Individuals nurtured on the concept of "everybody gets the same items" will often overlook this economic, yet powerful shortcut.

Once the test is originally devised, we would like to have procedures available for improving it. In a norm-referenced context we have available the time-honored devices such as item analyses techniques and reliability estimates which can guide us in test-refinement operations. With criterion-referenced measures, however, some of these classical constructs must be used differently. The next few sections of this paper will describe the nature of these differences.

Reliability

We all should know that for a single number to be used to describe the performance of a person on a test, the items on that test should all "measure the same thing" to some minimal extent. That is, the test should be internally consistent. This matter is treated in measurement texts in the chapter on reliability.

Now it is obvious that a criterion-referenced test should be internally consistent. If we argue that the items are tied to a criterion, then certainly the items should be quite similar in terms of what they are measuring. But although it may be obvious that a criterion-referenced test should be internally consistent, it is not obvious how to assess the internal consistency. The classical procedures are not appropriate. This is true because they are dependent on score variability. A criterion-referenced test should not be faulted if, when administered after instruction, everyone obtained a perfect score. Yet, that would lead to a zero internal-consistency estimate, something measurement books don't recommend.

In fact, even stranger things can happen in practice. It is possible for a criterion-referenced test to have a *negative* internal-consistency index and still be a good test. (See Husek and Sirotnik, 1968, for a more extensive treatment of this possibility.)

Thus, the typical indices of internal consistency are not appropriate for criterion-referenced tests. It is not clear what should replace them. Perhaps we need estimates, comparable to the standard internal-consistency formulas, which can take larger temporal units into consideration, for example, by considering both a pre-instruction test administration and a post-instruction test administration as part of the same extended phenomenon. Perhaps ingenious indices can be developed which reflect the ability of a test to produce variation from pre-instruction to post-instruction testing and, in these terms, internal consistency—despite score range restrictions. But until that time, those wishing to improve criterion-referenced tests should not be dismayed if the test, because of little score variance, yields a low internal-consistency estimate. It is really unwise to apply such estimates.

The foregoing discussion applies only to situations where the test is used to assess a single dimension, such as one instructional objective, as opposed to several dimensions, such as three very disparate objectives. If the objectives are substantially different, the items measuring them should be considered as different tests, not a single all-encompassing measure.

Other aspects of reliability are equally cloudy. Stability might certainly be important for a criterion-referenced test, but in that case, a test-retest correlation coefficient, dependent as it is on variability, is not necessarily the way to assess it. Some kind of confidence interval around the individual score is perhaps a partial solution to this problem.

The reader should not misinterpret the above statements. If a criterion-referenced test has a high average inter-item correlation, this is fine. If the test has a high test-retest correlation, that is also fine. The point is *not* that these indices cannot be used to support the consistency of the test. The point is that a criterion-referenced test could be highly consistent, either internally or temporarily, and yet indices dependent on variability might not reflect that consistency.

Validity

Many of the procedures for assessing the validity of norm-referenced tests are based on correlations and thus on variability. Hence, with validity, as with reliability, the results of the procedures are useful if they are positive, but not necessarily devastating if they are negative.

Criterion-referenced measures are validated primarily in terms of the adequacy with which they represent the criterion. Therefore, content validity approaches are more suited to such tests. A carefully made judgment, based on the test's apparent relevance to the behaviors legitimately inferable from those delimited by the criterion, is the general procedure for validating criterion-referenced measures.

Certainly, for both norm-referenced and criterion-referenced measures a test specialist might employ construct validity strategies to support the confidence he can give to his instruments. For example, we might wish to augment our confidence in a measure we were using as a proximate predictor (e.g., administered at the close of instruction) of some more distant criterion (e.g., occurring many years hence). If positive intercorrelations occur among several proximate predictors (of the same distant criterion) we could add to our understanding of whether a given proximate predictor was doing its job.

Item Analysis

Item-analysis procedures have traditionally been used with norm-referenced tests to identify those items that were not properly discriminating among individuals taking the test. For instance, in an achievement test an unsatisfactory item would be one which could not properly discriminate between the more and less knowledgeable learners (as reflected by total test performance). Non-discriminating items are usually those which are (a) too easy, (b) too hard, and/or (c) ambiguous.

For criterion-referenced tests the use of discrimination indices must be modified. An item which doesn't discriminate need not be eliminated. If it reflects an important attribute of the criterion, such an item should remain in the test. We might be interested in a "non-discriminating" item's ability to discriminate among *anyone,* e.g., its ability to discriminate between those individuals who have and those who haven't been exposed to instruction. But, just as in the case of reliability estimates, such indices are not currently available.

A positively discriminating item is just as respectable in a criterion-referenced test as it is in a norm-referenced test, but certainly not more so. In fact, the positively discriminating item may point to areas of instruction (if the criterion measure is assessing the effects of instruction) where the program is not succeeding well enough.

However, negatively discriminating items are treated exactly the same way in a criterion-referenced approach as they are in a norm-referenced approach. An item which discriminates negatively is one which, in an instructional context, is answered correctly more often by the less knowledgeable than by the more knowledgeable students. When one discovers a negative discriminator in his pool of criterion-referenced items, he should be suspicious of it and after more careful analysis can usually detect flaws in such an item.

Of course, discrimination indices are little more than warning flags, and one must still use common sense in weighing the worth of an item identified as a negative discriminator. It might be that some deficiencies in the instruction caused the result rather than any fault of the item. Yet, is is more likely that the item is deficient. For example, suppose that the negatively discriminating item was originally generated, along with nineteen other items, as a measure of a particular type of criterion behavior. Now in order for the item to yield a negative discrimination index there would first have to be variable subject performance. But in addition, more of those individuals who scored well on the total twenty-item test would have to miss the suspect item more frequently than those who scored badly on the total test. Under such circumstances it seems more likely that it is an item deficiency, rather than instructional deficiency, although the latter possibility should be kept in mind.

Is it worth the trouble? Since we are only concerned with the identification of negative discriminators, not non-discriminators, should criterion-referenced measures be subjected to item analysis operations? This would seem to depend on the ease with which one can conduct the necessary analyses. As data processing becomes increasingly automated and less expensive, such analyses would seem warranted in situations where the effort is not immense.

Reporting and Interpretation

We use norm-referenced and criterion-referenced tests to make decisions about both individuals and treatments. We need, therefore, to interpret test results properly in order to make the best possible decisions. With respect to norm-referenced measurement the methods of interpreting the results of an individual's test performance are well known. Since we are interested in an individual's performance with respect to the performance of other individuals, we use such group-relative descriptors as percentile rankings or standard scores. Such indices allow us to tell, from a single score, how well the individual performed in relationship to the group.

When interpreting an individual's performance on a criterion-referenced test, however, such group-relative indices are not appropriate. Some criterion-referenced tests yield scores which are essentially "on-off" in nature, that is, the individual has either mastered the criterion or he hasn't. For example, certain examinations in the chemistry laboratory may require a pupil to combine and treat chemical compounds in such a way that they produce hydrogen. In such tests it is sufficient to report whether or not the learner has displayed the desired criterion behavior.

More commonly, however, a range of acceptable performances exists. For example, suppose that an instrucional objective had been devised which required a learner to multiply correctly pairs of three digit numbers. We could prepare twenty items composed of randomly selected digits to measure this skill. Because of possible computation errors, the required proficiency level for each successful student might be set at 90 percent, or better, thereby allowing errors on two of the twenty items. In reporting an individual's performance on a test such as this, one alternative is to once more use an "on-off" approach, namely, either the 90 percent minimum has been achieved or it hasn't.

Whether we wish to report the degree of less-than-criterion performance should depend *exclusively* on the use we can make of the data. For example, if there are only two courses of action available to the individual, depending on his success or failure with respect to the criterion, then we need only report it as that, success or failure. However, if some differential experiences are to be provided on the basis of the degree of his less-than-criterion performance, then one would be interested in how far away he was from the criterion. For instance, if there were two remedial multiplication programs available, one for those very close to criterion and one for those who scored 60 percent or below on the twenty-item examination, then we would report the degree of his performance. The point is that such gradations in reporting are only a function of the alternative courses of action available to the individual after the measurement has been made.

With respect to the evaluation of treatments, it has already been pointed out that norm-referenced measures are not the most suitable devices for such purposes since their emphasis on producing heterogeneous performance sometimes diverts them from adequately reflecting the treatment's intended objectives. In using criterion-referenced measures for purposes of treatment assessment, *e.g.*, testing the merits of a

new set of programmed mathematics materials, we have several alternatives. We could simply report the number of individuals who achieve the
pre-established criterion. Although such a procedure seems to supply
scant data, it has the advantage of making graphically clear the proportion of learners who did not achieve criterion level proficiency. Too often
this result is masked through the use of statistical averages.

We could also use traditional descriptive statistics such as means
and standard deviations. Because one is often interested in the average
performance produced by a treatment, as well as its variability, such
statistics are useful. An average "percentage correct," however, is a helpful addition. Sometimes, if the criterion level for an individual has been
set as a particular level, it is useful to report the proportion of the group
which reached that level. For instance, using 80 percent as a criterion
level, then one might describe a group's performance as 92–80, indicating
that 92 percent of the group had achieved 80 percent or better on the test.
Such reporting, however, overlooks the proportion and degree of the
better-than-criterion performance. It would seem, then, that in using
criterion-referenced measures to make decisions about treatments, the
best course of action would be to employ a number of these schemes to
report the group's performance in order to permit more enlightened
interpretations.

Different Kinds of Criterion-Referenced Tests

Up to this point we have discussed criterion-referenced tests as if
there were one such animal. Actually, there are two. One could be said
to be the ideal case and the other the more typical case.

In the ideal case the items are not only tied to the criterion but, in
addition, the test is homogeneous in a very special sense. Everyone who
gets the same score on the test has obtained the score in essentially the
same manner. The meaning of a score is thus altogether unambiguous.
If we know a person's score we know his response pattern; we know
within error limits exactly what he can and cannot do. This would be an
ideal criterion-referenced test, since it not only eliminates the need for
a reference group but also immediately tells us the behavior repertoire
of the student for that criterion. This kind of test has been discussed in
the literature for some time. Guttman mentioned it as early as 1944 and
Tucker elaborated on the concept in 1952.

Unfortunately, this kind of test is still mostly a dream for educational testers. Since we need to know an immense amount about the
subject matter of the test, and perhaps even about the reasons why students make certain kinds of responses, these tests at the present time are
found only in relatively restricted and formal areas such as mathematics.

The other type of criterion-referenced test is more typical. The items on the test can be thought of as a sample from a potentially large group that might be generated from a criterion. The score on the test is not completely unambiguous; if we know that a student earned a score of 90 percent correct, we do not know which items he missed. However, we do know, if we have constructed our test properly, that of the items defining the criterion behavior the student missed only 10 percent. And if the test is homogeneous, this tells us a great deal about what the student can do.

The purpose of the foregoing discussion has been to draw distinctions between norm-referenced and criterion-referenced measurement with respect to several key measurement constructs. Because of the recency of its introduction into the field, criterion-referenced measurement received most attention. This should not imply any superiority of one approach over the other. Each has its relatively distinct role to play. The roles are only relatively distinct because one can usually employ a test developed for one purpose in another situation and still derive useful information from it. It seems, however, that there are some psychometric properties of these two types of measurement which render them most appropriate for the purposes for which they were originally designed.

References

CRONBACH, L.J., "Evaluation for Course Improvement." *Teachers College Record* 64 (1963), pp. 672–83.

CRONBACH, L.J., and G.C. GLESER, *Psychological Tests and Personnel Decisions*, 2nd ed. (Urbana, Ill.: University of Illinois Press, 1965).

GLASER, R., "Instructional Technology and the Measurement of Learning Outcomes: Some Questions." *American Psychologist* 18 (1963), pp. 519–21.

GUTTMAN, L., "A Basis for Scaling Qualitative Ideas." *American Sociological Review* 9 (1949), pp. 139–50.

HUSEK, T.R., and K. SIROTNIK, "Item Sampling in Educational Research: An Empirical Investigation." (Paper presented at the national meetings of the American Educational Research Association, Chicago, February, 1968. Available as NAPS Document 00255 from ASIS National Auxiliary Publications Service, care of CCM Information Sciences, Inc., 22 West 34th Street, New York, N.Y.).

LORD, F.M., and M.R. NOVICK, *Statistical Theories of Mental Test Scores* (Reading: Mass.: Addison-Wesley, 1968).

TUCKER, L., "Scales Minimizing the Importance of Reference Groups." In *Proceedings of the Invitational Conference on Testing Problems* (Princeton, N.J.: Educational Testing Service, 1952), pp. 22–28.

11

Program Fair Evaluation — Summative Assessment of Instructional Sequences with Dissimilar Objectives

As today's educational evaluators acquire increasing sophistication regarding the appraisal of instructional programs, they encounter classes of evaluation problems which promise to tax their expertise to its limits. Some of these problems are associated with relatively new issues, while others have been with us for many years. One question receiving considerable attention in the 1960's pertains to the comparative evaluation of two or more instructional sequences which have some objectives that are the same but some that are different.

, At first glance this would seem to be an age-old evaluation problem, since educators have had the problem of choosing among competing instructional sequences for many years. Yet, only recently has it been possible to apply much rigor to the task of choosing among instructional alternatives. This stems from a development in the field of instruction, namely, the tendency to prepare instructional sequences which are essentially *replicable* and which take responsibility for promoting specified changes in appropriate learners. In earlier days curriculum specialists usually designed what they hoped was an optimal instructional program, then evaluated it. Rarely did they have an opportunity to choose among competing instructional sequences. It was tough enough just to get one into operation. But today, due in part to the impact of the programmed instruction movement, more and more replicable instructional products are appearing on the educational market. These products range from short, one-lesson programs to elaborate, year-long packages. Their replicability qualities make it possible for school people to select a product and be relatively sure that it can be used in the local situation in much the same way that it was previously used·in other situations. Local curriculum

This article is based on a research memorandum prepared for the Southwest Regional Laboratory for Education Research and Development in 1968. Reprinted from *National Society for Programmed Instruction Journal*, July, 1969.

workers need not put up their own instructional preserves, they can now buy them at the market.

But as any housewife will tell you, comparative shopping is difficult. It's hard to decide which of two roasts to purchase when there are several differences between them, e.g., quality (prime versus choice), weight (4 lbs., 6 ozs., versus 5 lbs., 2 ozs.), bone content ("not much" versus "mostly marrow"). Decisions are particularly difficult when such differences do not uniformly favor one of the potential purchases. In the same way a consumer of educational products faces a complex problem when he is obliged to choose between two sets of instructional materials which, among other differences, are designed to promote goals that are, at least to some extent, dissimilar.

Let us consider, for example, an increasingly common kind of educational dilemma. A local school district curriculum committee has been commissioned to select a set of biology materials for use in the district's high schools. There are now several sets of such materials on the market, each with its own collection of texts, pupil work books, teacher manuals, etc. Because of careful structuring of the materials, it can be said they are essentially replicable, that is, can probably be used in roughly the same way by various biology instructors. Each of the three most eligible sets of materials has been field-tested to the point where there are data available regarding the degree to which each program can promote achievement of its objectives. The perplexity facing the curriculum committee, however, is that the objectives of the three programs differ. Even with a wealth of performance data regarding each program's effectiveness, the committee still must somehow reconcile the differences among the programs with respect to intended outcomes. This is a common instance of a summative evaluation task which will be presented to educators with increasing frequency as a consequence of the expanding availability of replicable instructional products (Scriven, 1967). How should such a problem best be resolved?

There are a number of approaches which can be used, ranging from the crude to the complex. A proposal will be forwarded later which, it is hoped, is (1) sufficiently practicable so that it can be readily used and (2) sufficiently sensitive so that it yields the appropriate information for evaluative decisions. But first let's dispense with some of the more simplistic evaluation strategies which have, unfortunately, been used all too often in comparing instructional sequences with differing objectives.

It should be noted at the outset that this discussion pertains to comparative evaluations (i.e., making judgments as to which of two or more contenders is *better*) of any types of instructional sequences that yield essentially replicable instructional events. For example, this would include sets of self-instruction programs in which a "live" teacher plays little or no role. It would also pertain to instructional sequences in which teachers are heavily involved but influenced in one or more ways so that they produce a form of instruction which is largely the same from one group of learners to the next. It obviously doesn't make much sense to devote intense evaluation efforts to contrasts of non-replicable instruction, such as that spontaneously generated by "off-the-cuff" teachers whose performance is so variable that generalizations regarding future instruction are risky. So we are talking here about comparative evaluations of such entities as long-term national curriculum projects which yield fairly reliable instruction (perhaps because they are largely material-based) or short-term instructional sequences such as the teacher's use of highly prescriptive lesson plans, unit plans, etc.

One comparative evaluation strategy has found evaluators responding exclusively to "presentation" stimuli which may or may not be related to student attainment of instructional objectives. How many times, for instance, have educators chosen one set of reading materials over another because of such packaging factors as the quality of illustrations, covers, attractiveness of page make-up, etc.? Not that such things are necessarily irrelevant to learner achievements, it's just that they usually have not been demonstrated to be germane. Or, again, we find some educators preferring one program to another primarily because they are impressed with an author's style or the way he treats a particular concept. Such approaches never raise the really important question of *"What happens to the learner as a consequence of his encounter with the instructional sequences?"* Of course style and treatment of content may be critically related to learner post-instruction behavior. But such relationships are rarely, if ever, verified. Instead the evaluator trusts his intuition regarding the probable impact of such factors. Intuitively derived evaluations such as these are difficult to defend.

A more reasonable approach to cross-program evaluation involves the use of learner performance measures. A common practice has been to administer either a standardized achievement test or a specially constructed achievement test to learners who have completed different instructional sequences, then compare their respective performances on that measure. The weakness with such approaches, however, is that such tests often lack sufficient relevance to the objectives of either program. A standardized test, for example, is usually developed in a *norm-referenced* context where the primary purpose of the test is to differentiate among individuals, rather than a *criterion-referenced* context where the primary purpose of the test is to assess the degree to which an individual has achieved a criterion (Glaser, 1963). Because of the procedures associated with the development and refinement of norm-referenced measures, e.g., item analysis and the quest for highly variant scores, such tests often fail to retain items which assess truly important outcomes of given instructional programs. Therefore, to use them as a principal basis for judgment may obscure the true effectiveness of the program in question.

In somewhat the same way a specially designed test which is used to assess the merits of two or more discrete instructional programs often suffers from attempting to serve multiple masters. By trying to cover fairly the objectives of more than one program, the resulting test is often a watered-down instrument which tells the evaluator little. Even worse, such a test may inadvertently place greater emphasis on the objectives of one program, thereby favoring it when learner performance is evaluated.

Although these two approaches, namely, the use of criteria other than learner behavior and the use of a single test, have been the most widely employed procedures for comparing two or more instructional programs with different objectives, there are other, less common strategies. Wolf (1968) has recently described these and has identified weaknesses in each.

Program Fair Evaluation

The proposed scheme for avoiding some of the previously identified weaknesses is both conceptually simple and easy to implement. For ease of exposition, a comparative evaluation involving only two instructional sequences will be considered, although it is clear that the approach can be extended to comparisons involving more than two programs. For a hypothetical case, consider the problem faced by an evaluator who must choose between Program X and Program Y which have some objectives that are the same and some objectives that are different.

To devise an evaluation scheme which will be fair to both programs, the evaluator should first isolate the instructional objectives for each of the two programs. If the objectives are not presented by the programs' developers, it may be necessary to infer them from the programs' criterion tests or, lacking these, from the programs themselves (Popham, 1964). To be of any help to the evaluator, such objectives must, of course, be stated operationally in terms of intended learner behavior changes. Loose, global objectives are of little utility at this point. Having identified each program's objectives, they should then be grouped, as indicated in Figure 1, into those common to both programs, those unique to Program X, and those unique to Program Y.

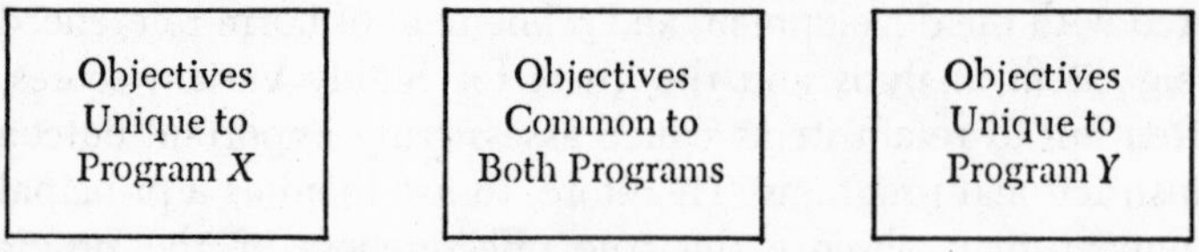

Objectives Unique to Program X	Objectives Common to Both Programs	Objectives Unique to Program Y

FIGURE 1. A Classification of Objectives for Program X and Program Y.

In performing this first operation, that is, isolating the unique and the common objectives, it may be possible to work exclusively from test items rather than objectives. There would seem, however, to be some advantage in having the objectives clearly before us since by examining these we could more easily see the class of test items covered and could more readily identify whether a test item should be used for a particular program.

Once the objectives have been classified as common or unique to one of the two programs, representative tests of each of the three sets of objectives must be generated. And "test" here is used broadly, in the sense that one could generate written and non-written measures for objectives in the affective domain as well as the cognitive. Ideally, we would like to have an equitable proportion of test items based on the objectives involved, though by no means does this imply three tests of equal length. For example, if the situation presented in Figure 2 prevailed, where one of the sets of unique objectives was much larger than the other unique set, we would probably have about twice as many test items for objectives unique to Program X as for objectives unique to Program Y. This is complicated, unfortunately, by the fact that to gauge reliably whether learners can perform certain objectives may take only a single or very few items, while other objectives require a larger number of items. Thus, in the hypothetical situation depicted in Figure 2 it is conceivable that the four objectives peculiar to Program Y might actually require more items than the nine objectives peculiar to Program X. More commonly, however, the number of test items required by the three sets of objectives will be proportional to the number of objectives in the three categories. In any case, the evaluator must decide how many items per objective are required to provide a reasonable index of whether the learner has achieved that particular objective.

FIGURE 2. A Hypothetical Classification of Program Objectives.

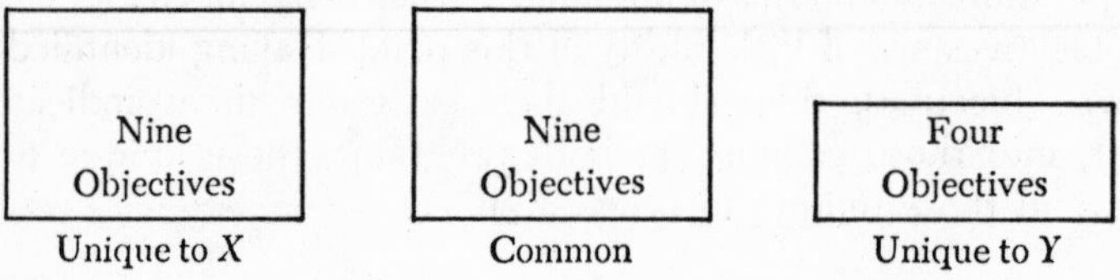

Nine Objectives	Nine Objectives	Four Objectives
Unique to X	Common	Unique to Y

The next task is to combine these three pools of items into a three-part examination which will subsequently be administered to learners who have completed only Program X and to learners who have completed only Program Y. There are several methods by which this three-part test can be constructed. One would be to present in discrete sections first the set of common items, then the items unique to the program the learner had completed, then the items unique to the program he had not completed. A second approach would be to order randomly the items from all three sets. The writer favors the latter approach, although there is a possibility that the effect of the learner's encountering test items (during the course of completing the examination) with which he was completely unfamiliar might distort his overall performance. This would be avoided, of course, by appending the items unique to the uncompleted programs as the last section of the exam. One suspects, however, that test directions to the learner which included phrases such as the following would handle that difficulty: "In the test you are about to take, you will encounter some items with which you will not be familiar. Do as well as you can on such items, but do not be concerned by them. It is expected that you will not be able to answer some of the items in the examination." At any rate, this is a routine procedural question which can be readily answered through empirical investigations.

The next step in program fair evaluation is to assign values to the three sets of objectives. This, of course, is sticky business and it would be pleasant to avoid value judgments altogether because they are so subjective, imprecise, etc. Unfortunately, we can't. At this point the evaluator must reach a position, as clearly as possible, regarding the respective worth of the three sets of objectives. Ideally, the relative value of the three sets of objectives could even be quantified. For example, on a ten-point scale one could value the common objectives at eight, the objectives unique to Program X at four, and the objectives unique to Program Y at six. Undoubtedly, there are far more sensitive procedures for translating one's value appraisals into indices which incorporate differential estimates of the worth of objectives. For instance, one could assign a numerical value index to each objective, whether common or unique. But it would be helpful at this stage even to make a gross commitment where the evaluator might assert that "Objectives unique to Program X are more important than the common objectives. Further, the common objectives are more important than those unique to Program Y."

Next, a sample of appropriate learners is randomly assigned to one of the two instructional treatments and, after they have completed their respective sequences, are given the three-part criterion test. We are assuming that the average time taken to complete each program is com-

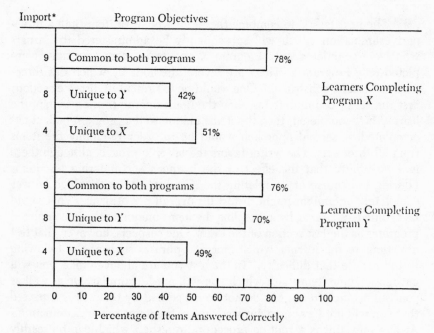

*Estimated on a 1–10 scale, 10 = Very Important

FIGURE 3. Hypothetical Results of Two Groups of Learners
Completing Two Different Programs.

parable, although adjustments could be made in criterion test scores if one program took much longer to complete than the other.

Finally, based on the performance of the two groups of learners on the three subtests, and taking cognizance of the previously judged worth of each set of objectives, a comparative evaluation is made whereby one of the two programs is selected. For example, suppose the results depicted in Figure 3 had occurred, what kind of decision should be reached (other factors being equal)?

It would seem that because the objectives unique to Program Y were considered so important (eight on a 10 point scale), that Program Y would be selected here. Both programs yield learner performance on the other two sets of objectives which, though favoring Program X, are roughly comparable. Program Y produces clearly superior results on objectives unique to itself while doing almost as well as Program X on the other two dimensions.

Of course, one could generate other fictitious sets of results where the decision-maker would face a more difficult choice. Considering value weightings and relative success of learners on the three sets of objectives, there might be situations presented where the evaluator would resort to a coin flip. But even the most elaborate evaluation scheme will occasionally yield such impasses. The value of the procedure described here is that it can sharpen the evaluator's awareness of the degree to which different instructional sequences are performing different kinds of jobs.

Results on such an examination must be weighed, of course, along with other important factors such as cost, re-usability of materials, teacher attitudes toward the programs, etc. But assuming such factors are relatively equal, appraisal of results such as those included in Figure 3 should aid the evaluator.

Recapitulating, then, the steps involved in conducting a program fair evaluation of two instructional programs are the following:

1. Identify objectives (a) common to both programs, (b) unique to one program, and (c) unique to the other program.

2. Collect or construct test items based on the three sets of objectives.

3. Combine the test items into a three-part examination.

4. Assign estimates of importance, as explicitly as possible, to the three sets of objectives.

5. Administer each of the instructional programs to one of two randomly selected groups of appropriate learners.

6. Administer the three-part examination to both groups.

7. Appraise results and reach a decision regarding the preferred program.

The summative evaluation scheme described here for comparing programs with dissimilar objectives is relatively straightforward and can, therefore, be carried out with little difficulty. It can be applied to the evaluation of short-duration instructional sequences or to programs of much greater magnitude. While conceptually simple, it provides the evaluator with opportunities, if he wishes, to employ sophisticated quantification schemes to deal with such problems as value weightings of objectives. The major purpose of the procedure, of course, is to make evaluators attentive to the differential consequences of employing instructional programs which were designed with different intentions.

References

GLASER, ROBERT, "Instructional Technology and the Measurement of Learning Outcomes: Some Questions." *American Psychologist* 18 (1963), pp. 519–21.

Popham, W. James, "A Comparison of Rough and Dirty Methods of Evaluating Self-Instruction Programs." (Working paper, UCLA Program Effectiveness Project, October, 1964.)

Scriven, Michael, "The Methodology of Evaluation." In B.O. Smith, ed., *Perspectives of Curriculum Evaluation* (Chicago: Rand McNally, 1967).

Wolf, Richard, "Program Free Testing." (Research Memorandum, Southwest Regional Laboratory for Educational Research and Development, Inglewood, California, May, 1968.)

PART FIVE
Selecting Objectives as an Alternative to Generating Objectives

The two selections in this section describe an alternative procedure for having teachers organize their instructional thinking around statements of measurable objectives, yet not obliging those teachers to spend hours churning out such statements. The initial selection offers a rationale for the Instructional Objectives Exchange as an example of an agency from which objectives can be selected for local use by educators. The second selection traces the early history of the Exchange.

12

The Instructional Objectives Exchange:
New Support for Criterion-Referenced
Instruction

"The quality of any instructional sequence must be evaluated primarily in terms of its ability to promote desirable changes in the intended learner." This assertion, or statements similar to it, have met with the increasing approval of influential American educators during recent years. Not that it represents a novel conception—one could undoubtedly locate comparable utterances from the very beginnings of educational history. But the increasingly widespread agreement with this conception of instructional effectiveness is new.

Criterion-Referenced Instruction

Perhaps the type of instructional strategy being advocated these days can best be described as *criterion-referenced instruction*. This approach focuses primarily on the degree to which the learner can perform specified criterion behaviors. For example, in preparing instructional materials, the developers decide what to revise according to learner performance data, not according to the judgment of consulting experts. In another situation, a school district selects one set of supplementary reading texts instead of another because of pupil performance on related criterion tests, not because one set of texts is more attractively illustrated than the other. Such examples accurately suggest that a primary feature of criterion-referenced instruction is a preoccupation with the results of instruction, not the procedures used to promote them. It is an ends-oriented approach to instruction rather than a means-oriented approach. Since most educators concur that the ultimate index of an educational

This article is based on a symposium presentation at the annual meeting of the American Educational Research Association in Los Angeles, February, 1969. It is reprinted from the November, 1970, issue of *Phi Delta Kappan*. Copyright 1970 by Phi Delta Kappa, Inc.

program's worth is the degree to which it benefits the learner, the increased support of criterion-referenced instructional approaches is gratifying.

But against the increasingly supportive backdrop, it is distressing that very few large-scale criterion-referenced instructional operations are under way. Verbal support is there. But there is not yet widespread practical implementation. Why?

The principal deterrent to the spread of criterion-referenced approaches is fairly easy to identify. Developing criterion measures of sufficient quality and satisfactory breadth is too much work for most educators.

Much of the recent agitation regarding the desirability of describing instructional objectives in terms of measurable learner behavior is based on the belief that the impact of instruction can be more readily assessed by operationally stated objectives. Many proponents of operationally stated educational objectives are beginning to complain about the paucity of such objectives in the schools. Educators can be taught to state objectives properly; they can even become quite enthusiastic about the desirability of stating them behaviorally. But few of them do it. Teachers are already too burdened to find the time to develop operationally stated objectives for their classes. School districts have already committed their increasingly limited resources to other tasks. In those isolated instances where there has been an effort to develop precise instructional objectives on a large scale, the participating educators will readily admit how taxing the enterprise has been. Financial and personnel costs point up another problem. In spite of the difficulties, some districts are undertaking the task. For example, the Clark County (Nevada) School District developed a set of behaviorally stated objectives for mathematics instruction in grades K-6. There are other examples of such endeavors in various parts of the U.S.

The absence of any scheme to acquaint districts with other developmental projects makes it probable that a distressing amount of duplication will occur. For instance, more than a year after the Clark County, Nevada, schools had completed their preparation of K-6 instructional objectives for mathematics, two districts in different states commenced work on precisely the same project, unaware of the Clark County objectives. The wheel was about to be re-invented.

Objective Selection

It may be expecting too much to ask already harassed teachers and administrators to generate their own objectives. But though *objective generation* may be too demanding, *objective selection* should not be. If the instructor's task were simply to choose from comprehensive sets of operationally stated objectives those which he wished to achieve, his task would be manageable. He could follow through on his commitments to precisely explicated goals without being obliged to construct them himself.

When the educator is the selector rather than the generator of objectives, there may be some concern regarding the degree to which the objectives will be "imposed from above." A viable objectives selection scheme, however, should permit just that—the *selection* of objectives. If all of the objectives which the selector favors are not available, he can always generate more. Local autonomy in the selection of objectives should be an integral part of any scheme. Objectives should increase the educator's range of alternatives, never decrease his self-direction.

Objectives Plus Criterion Measures

Precise objectives may be. necessary, but by themselves they are far from sufficient. Too often even a behaviorally stated objective may be used as window dressing for "instruction as usual." A precise objective can be most helpful when planning an instructional sequence, but it becomes even more useful for evaluating one. To what degree has the objective been achieved? The answer can be given only by measuring devices based explicitly on the objective.

Few districts have made the logical jump from developing objectives to developing test items. "Test items" include observation of learner behaviors reflecting cognitive as well as noncognitive outcomes. If a school district had access to sets of objectives plus test items, it could readily assess the degree to which its instructional approaches were successful. The existence of a pool of test items for each objective would encourage educators throughout the nation to initiate criterion-referenced instructional strategies.

The Instructional Objectives Exchange

To this end, the UCLA Center for the Study of Evaluation established the Instructional Objectives Exchange in 1968 as a national depository and development agency for instructional objectives and related measurement devices. The exchange will perform the following functions:

1. It will serve as a visible clearinghouse to keep abreast of the instructional objectives projects throughout the nation.

2. It will provide a bank-like agency where a school district (or

comparable educational agency) can "draw out" all the objectives and relevant measures for as many subjects, grades, topics, etc., as desired.

3. It will continually update, refine, and expand the pool of objectives and measures for each field covered by the exchange.

The potential impact of such an exchange, readily providing pools of objectives and test items from which districts can select, should not be underestimated. With competent staffing, a careful developmental plan, and proper dissemination strategies, the exchange could conceivably alter the nature of instructional practice in America.

Operation of the Exchange

Briefly, this is how the exchange will function. First, we will attempt to make as many educators as possible aware of the existence of the exchange and the service it provides. We have already distributed nationally news releases, magazine articles, letters to school districts, and descriptive brochures. Contained in this literature describing the exchange is a request that any school district or comparable agency which has developed behaviorally stated instructional objectives contribute these to the exchange. While it is too early yet to say how many collections of behaviorally stated objectives exist throughout the country, there are encouraging indications that there may have been more projects focused on the development of precise objectives than we had anticipated.

As this collection activity progresses, the staff of the exchange will concurrently be developing objectives and related item pools, particularly in those areas where we find few satisfactorily stated objectives. We are now refining our procedures for developing properly stated objectives and criterion-referenced items which accurately reflect the attainment of such objectives. Although our early efforts have quite naturally found us emphasizing cognitive objectives, we hope to soon move to the development of a variety of noncognitive goals.

In early 1970 the Instructional Objectives Exchange separated from the Center for the Study of Evaluation and is now a nonprofit educational corporation. Currently, thirty-five separate collections of objectives are available from the exchange covering a wide range of subjects in grades K–12. Most of these objectives are accocpanied by six test items which may be used to measure whether the objectives have been achieved. Although the bulk of these thirty-five collections are focused on cognitive outcomes, two sets of objectives deal exclusively with affective outcomes, i.e., learners' self-concepts and attitudes toward school.

13

Potential Uses of IOX Objectives

The general conception of instruction endorsed by the Instructional Objectives Exchange (IOX) is that instructional improvement is facilitated by clear definition of desired instructional outcomes and the subsequent measurement of post-instruction learner attainment of those outcomes.

Many school personnel who are sympathetic to the general goals of IOX recognize that educational innovations are often misunderstood, and consequently resisted, by potential users. These educators suggested, therefore, that we prepare something comparable to a "resource unit," consisting of many possible ways to use the materials available from IOX. This compilation of possible activities is a response to that suggestion.

These suggestions are offered as *alternatives,* not prescriptions. Any school or school district might use as few or as many of these activities as it wishes. The wide variety of procedures should make clear that there are a number of possible ways in which objectives can effectively be used. These alternatives reflect the underlying IOX theme: *a commitment to the desirability of well-defined instructional goals and to objective-based evaluation.* In keeping with that philosophy, the suggested uses are biased in favor of assessing the quality of instruction in terms of measurable learner growth.

Because the use of a bank of instructional objectives represents a significant departure for many teachers, careful consideration should be given to the recommended plans for initiating changes. For example, it would be imprudent for an administrator to force teachers, who are otherwise uninformed, to choose from objectives in the IOX collections. Clearly, teaching personnel, supervisors, administrators, and related educational personnel should be partners in this enterprise.

Selecting Objectives

Collections from the Instructional Objectives Exchange can be used either by an individual teacher or a group of teachers, such as a departmental faculty. For example, after examining the available objectives, an individual teacher will undoubtedly discover some that he will wish to adopt for his students. These might be used either as a *total*, a *minimal*, or a *partial* set of goals for the class. It is conceivable, of course, that objectives other than those contained in the IOX materials might be taught concurrently with the IOX objectives. Teachers may, therefore, consider IOX objectives as a minimal set of objectives for their classes.

Because different teachers have different preferences, a group of teachers in the same subject or grade level, for example, the faculty of a high school English department, might jointly identify those objectives that were approved by all, or almost all, of the teachers. These objectives could be useful in assessing across-the-board departmental attainment of objectives through the use of pre-test and post-test measures of the objectives. An item-sampling procedure, in which different students in various classes complete different items, could also be used, thereby making cross-class or cross-individual comparisons less likely.

It is also possible for students to participate in the selection of the objectives for their own educational programs. The advantages of student involvement in the selection of objectives have been described by a number of writers. Students can be taught, depending upon their level of maturity, to consider the range of objectives in an IOX Collection and indicate those which they think would be most appropriate for their own instruction. As a basis for selecting objectives, student preferences can be used as the sole source of selection or they can be combined with teacher preferences.

In addition, students could be taught to generate properly stated objectives other than those available in the Collections. They could then be given the opportunity to generate such objectives. Their familiarity with the requirements of measurable objectives could beneficially affect their interaction with an instructional system designed to promote such goals.

Learner participation in the selection of objectives might be particularly appropriate for disadvantaged students who have been discouraged by customary school instruction. Giving them an opportunity to play a role in the selection of their own instructional goals could result in greater involvement and subsequent learning success for such students.

Another way to select objectives is to assess community preferences in terms of what ought to be taught in the schools. A representative group of citizens might be invited to consider objectives in one or more Collections and then be interviewed to determine which objectives they judge most important, next most important, and so on. An actual ranking system of objectives (first choice, second choice, and so forth) could be employed. The same plan might be carried out on a less personal basis through the use of mailed questionnaires.

The preferences of members of the local school board should also be given serious consideration. These preferences could be determined by interviews or by referring to the overall instructional objectives of the school board if they are available.

Rather than undertaking individual projects to assess the needs of pupils, citizens, and faculty, users of the IOX objectives might undertake a more comprehensive assessment of instructional needs by pooling data from all three sources and then comparing the preferences of these groups. Interviews might be conducted with appropriately sampled representatives of the faculty, the community, and the student clientele. These individuals could be asked to rank the objectives listed in one or more of the IOX Collections, and the rankings could then be compared and interpreted.

Such a comprehensive assessment of needs would undoubtedly yield a better indication of desirable objectives than would a less complete data-gathering technique. The sophistication of the needs-assessment operation will depend, of course, on the resources available to those conducting the operation. More sophisticated plans will involve the stratification of the various groups from which data are secured.

Individual teachers or school faculties may certainly wish to generate operationally stated objectives for those areas where none exist. For example, if objectives a teacher considers important are not included in the current Collection, he could generate such objectives, and even sample items, to meet that need.

Instruction

In addition to the Collections of instructional objectives available to teachers, a teacher should ideally have a bank of instructional means or procedures to use with those objectives. Having selected instructional objectives from among alternatives, he would like to be able to select instructional means that have a high probability of accomplishing those objectives. Unfortunately, this need cannot be met at this time.

Some research-and-development agencies are working on this problem and they hope to be able to provide recommendations on sound procedures or material to meet given goals. For the foreseeable future, however, the teacher will either have to generate his own instructional plans or identify extant instructional materials and procedures.

Although this situation may seem distressing, there is an extremely important advantage in having teachers assess the degree to which current objectives are being achieved. It is probable that a number of objectives now thought to be effectively accomplished by the schools will, upon assessment, prove to be unachieved. The mere realization that an intended set of outcomes is not being attained may, and certainly should, stimulate the instructional staff to undertake alternative procedures. This "reappraisal potential" of the Instructional Objectives Exchange should not be underestimated, for it can stimulate the educator to investigate different, hopefully improved, instructional plans.

It must be made clear that an instructor using the IOX objectives need not select items for an entire semester or an academic year. It is quite possible to select objectives for a teaching unit of only a few weeks' duration or for a single lesson. Instruction can be designed to accomplish objectives that seem achievable in any given period of time. Early attempts to utilize IOX materials might profitably focus on short periods of instruction.

Although it would require much planning time, the development of an individualized set of objectives for each child is certainly made possible by IOX objectives and test measures.

A comprehensive pre-test covering a wide range of objectives considered desirable by the teacher could be given to all students. A different set of objectives could be selected for each student on the basis of that student's mastery of the total objectives displayed in the pre-test. Individual progress toward the objectives could be made by students through the use of textbooks, self-instruction materials, small-group work, teacher direction, and so on. Ideally, as the school year passes, an individual student could monitor his own progress toward the achievement of his particular set of objectives.

There are some real advantages in employing contingency management plans in which certain rewards are offered to students on the basis of the degree to which they achieve their own objectives.

One of the advantages of using precisely stated objectives is that they can be communicated to the learner. A number of studies demonstrate that learners who have been informed of the teacher's instructional intentions can far more readily accomplish those goals.

For younger learners, the objectives may have to be modified so that they can be conveyed to the students in understandable language.

For more mature students, the selected set of objectives may be communicated early in the instructional program, or periodically, whichever the teacher considers to be more appropriate. Certain objectives, such as those in the affective domain, might not be given to students if knowledge of the objectives would be expected to influence adversely the degree to which the attainment of the objectives can be validly measured. For instance, the student's knowledge of an affective objective related to good sportsmanship might encourage him to behave "for the teacher's benefit."

Instructional supervisors should, if possible, be involved in the process of selecting and achieving objectives in such a way that their supervisory efforts will be directed toward the more efficient achievement of such goals. Supervisors should be urged to identify the teachers' objectives and to determine the degree to which evidence of achievement has been gathered.

If possible, teachers should assess their learners' attainment of an objective while there is still some instructional time to work toward unachieved goals. By using a *criterion check,* that is, a check of the learner's mastery of criterion behaviors (objectives) before the final examination, teachers can recycle instruction to attain unachieved objectives. By drawing items from the item pools supplied with most IOX objectives, such a criteria check can be readily assembled.

Because the pupil's home environment can greatly influence his learning achievement, the objectives selected from an IOX Collection might be sent home for the parents' information and, hopefully, supportive interest.

If several teachers are attempting to achieve the same objectives, post-instruction sessions can be set aside for (1) an examination of evidence regarding the attainment of such objectives and (2) clinical discussions of the adequacy of certain procedures in promoting learner attainment of the goals. Remedies for problems must be found, particularly for unachieved objectives. Teachers who have been successful in achieving the objectives can share their methods with others.

If time permits, the instructional staff might conduct small-scale experimental studies in which specific hypotheses regarding the attainment of objectives are tested. As we have previously suggested, the effectiveness of differing sequences of objectives or en route behaviors might be tested with different groups of pupils. Subsequent judgments could then be made on the effectiveness of the several methods.

Some teachers may choose to attempt to correlate available tests and other instructional materials with the particular objectives they are using. Such activities would greatly simplify the instructional tasks of other teachers. Indeed, such correlations might be shared with teachers in other schools or school districts, thereby providing a teacher with several references to relevant instructional materials for the objectives he selects.

Another activity in which teachers might profitably engage is to build practice exercises for the terminal and en route behaviors they have selected. In some cases, these practice exercises may exist in available texts or teacher manuals, but in other situations the teacher will have to construct them. Results of this activity also might be shared with other teachers.

Evaluation

For some of the IOX Collections a sufficient number of test items does not currently exist. Several Collections contain only one sample test item for each objective. Additional test items could certainly be generated in order to assess the attainment of the objectives. The addition of such items would greatly facilitate the work of the IOX.

IOX objectives are screened by relatively primitive quality control devices to judge the worth of the numerous objectives. Interested educators could greatly increase the value of the objectives by exploring and developing alternative ways of judging the quality of those goals.

Which are the truly worthwhile objectives? Upon what bases are decisions made regarding the worth of such goals? Information pertinent to such questions would be of interest to all IOX participants.

Objectives that are appropriate for certain textbooks or other instructional materials might form the basis of a comparative evaluation of competing instructional products. For instance, if a district is considering which one of two sets of mathematics texts to select, a small-scale evaluation could be undertaken to provide data that would be useful in making a decision. Two groups of randomly selected learners could complete the alternative tests, then display relative mastery of the objectives through use of the appropriate IOX test items.

There is a growing trend to involve students in the evaluation of the proficiency of an instructional staff. Student rating forms and faculty evaluation booklets are widely used. If a school faculty wishes to employ student rating procedures, one helpful way of sharpening the relevance of learner ratings would be to have teachers inform the students of the course objectives, then request a rating of teaching skill. The student rater's focus might thus be directed toward the course goals rather than less relevant factors.

PART SIX

An Objectives-Based Strategy for Assessing Teacher Competence

A final application of instructional objectives is examined in this section through three essays which (1) offer the rationale for using teaching-performance tests as an index of the instructor's ability to accomplish pre-specified objectives, (2) describe early research conducted in an effort to validate this approach to teacher evaluation, and (3) summarize in less technical fashion the implication of such a strategy for teacher appraisal.

14

The Performance Test: A New Approach to the Assessment of Teaching Proficiency

There is no necessity to document the need for reliable measures of teaching proficiency. In almost unlimited instances, educators, particularly teacher educators, could profit enormously if valid indices of teaching effectiveness were available. It is partly because of this tremendous need that one despairs when surveying the advances made by researchers who have worked in the area of teacher-competence assessment during the past sixty years. The distressing truth is that we have not moved very far forward in our efforts to develop reliable measures of teacher effectiveness.

There is general agreement that the ultimate criterion of teacher competence should be pupil growth, and we have witnessed innumerable efforts to predict such growth through the use of systematic observations and ratings of teaching behavior. Countless hours have been devoted since the turn of the century to the careful observation and categorization of what teachers do in the classroom. In recent years, the sophistication with which observers have attacked classroom problems is almost frightening: observation schemes and explanatory constructs have become so multidimensional that the classroom observer may soon be forced to choose among several hundred descriptive dimensions every few milliseconds. Rating scales, too, have become more and more complicated, and we find increasing effort devoted to the analysis of increasingly smaller aspects of the teacher's performance.

In essence, the most commonly used measures of teacher effectiveness are attempts to mirror in some way the teacher's probable success in promoting learner achievement. Such procedures as ratings and

Reprinted from the Summer, 1968, issue of the *Journal of Teacher Education*, Vol. XIX, No. 2, p. 216.

checklists are generally conceded to be estimates, albeit very gross, of the teacher's ability to promote learner growth. The problem with such measures is that learner growth may be directed toward extremely different ends: different teachers may have markedly divergent goals in mind for their students. Therefore, when an evaluator such as a principal or supervisor observes a teacher in action and gives him a rating, it is usually the evaluator who is implicitly imposing his own conception of what the teacher's goals should be at the time the rating is made, even though they may, in fact, differ considerably from his own.

A second, more common situation occurs when a rater is concerned only with the instructional means the teacher employs, without any explicit consideration of the ends he is trying to achieve. In such instances, the evaluator may still rate the teacher according to his own very personal conception of the form classroom activities should take; but even here, the evaluator's standards of desirable classroom procedures will be inextricably tied to his notions, however cloudy, of what the *outcomes* of instruction should be. Therefore, it is not surprising that ratings, checklists, and other comparable approaches have yielded very unsatisfactory results with respect to the assessment of teacher competence. McNeil[1] has enumerated the problems encountered because of the tendency of evaluators to impose their own value systems on teachers, even though they may use supposedly neutral measurement devices.

Faced with the complexities resulting from divergent instructional objectives, those researchers studying classroom teaching procedures make a very critical mistake when they attempt to ferret out supposedly superior instructional procedures that could be used with equal efficacy by different teachers. Most experienced researchers in this field now recognize that the quality of learning in a given instructional situation is the result of *particular* instructional procedures employed by a *particular* instructor for *particular* students with *particular* goals in mind. In other words, although the instructional *means* may vary considerably from teacher to teacher, both may accomplish identical *ends* with equal success.

Why not turn directly to measures of pupil growth in an effort to void this problem? Once again we encounter teachers' commitments to dissimilar objectives, which make it difficult to apply evaluation devices such as standardized achievement tests. The comprehensive nature of standardized measures often obscures the very important differential emphases made by teachers during the instructional process.

At UCLA we are adopting a different approach to this assessment dilemma.[2] We propose to circumvent the good-teaching-procedures question and use only pupil growth as a criterion. For the present, we are willing to overlook the question of how teachers achieve pupil gain. We recognize that because of fantastic personal variation among teachers extremely different procedures may work, even when "work" is defined in terms of pupil's achieving precisely the same objectives. We certainly believe that researchers should continue their efforts to discover which instructional techniques have a high probability of achieving instructional ends, but for the moment, we shall simply sidestep the question of what those techniques are.

Our assumption is that the teacher who is the better achiever of *given* instructional goals will, other factors being relatively equal, be the better achiever of his own goals. We therefore are developing tests of teaching performance wherein the teacher is given sets of explicit instructional objectives, asked to teach specifically to them, and has his competence assessed in terms of his ability to produce the pupil behavior changes described by those objectives.

A series of performance tests of instructor competence are being developed by UCLA under provision of two USOE contracts. Two of the tests are in the field of vocational education and one is in the social sciences. These tests consist of (1) a set of operational instructional objectives stated in terms of specific pupil behaviors, (2) a collection of possible learning activities a teacher may wish to employ, and (3) pre-tests and post-tests, not seen or administered by the teacher, that adhere closely to the operational objectives. The objectives and possible activities are given to the teacher one week in advance of instruction, and he is told to prepare plans for two weeks of teaching. Members of the project staff administer the pre-tests and post-tests to the teacher's pupils, and their progress toward the objectives serves as an index of the teacher's proficiency. By stipulating identical objectives to be achieved but permitting teacher diversity in the means used to accomplish these ends, a method of evaluating teaching performance is provided without restricting individualistic teaching style.

There are several theoretical problems associated with this particular approach to teacher-competence assessment, one of the most important of which concerns the validation of the performance tests to be developed. Our plan is to attempt, at the end of approximately two years, a validation wherein the performance of nonteachers (housewives, for example) is pitted against that of experienced teachers. The validation hypothesis will predict that the experienced teachers will secure better pupil achievement than will the nonteachers. This particular hypothesis, of course, is an extremely gross test, in that we wish to secure a marked contrast between (1) those who have never taught, and (2) those who have taught for some time (and in addition have been judged superior by administrators and supervisory personnel).

One of the problems is to obtain truly "good" teachers for this kind of contrast. Will teachers who have been selected by superiors as good instructors, even with respect to their previous records in promoting pupil achievement, be suitable for our purposes? Can we, in fact, hope for differences between these two groups; or like so many previous researchers, shall we be thwarted in the end by the very inexactness of the administrative ratings we ultimately hope to do away with? True, we do not plan to use administrative ratings as the competence criterion, but our validation scheme does involve the administrator's ability to select from experienced teachers a group of instructors who will be considerably better than nonteachers. Maybe this is asking too much.

There are other problems associated with the sensitivity of the tests we develop. Can pre-tests and post-tests based on the operational objectives be made sufficiently reliable and discriminating to serve our purposes? A very early field trial of one of the performance tests revealed scant differences between instructors who were teaching classes at very different levels of advancement in a junior college vocational program. If we cannot secure performance differences between such markedly different classes, surely our efforts are to be in vain. Furthermore, it is unlikely that tests yielding only statistical significance will be of any practical value in teacher-competence assessment. We need to develop much more dramatic ways of discriminating between teachers.

Another difficulty is associated with the attitudes of teachers toward the particular objectives selected. We will certainly make every effort to select instructional objectives that are approved by the teachers in the field, but undoubtedly there will be differences in the way these objectives are received. Perhaps we can control the differences in part by administering preinstruction attitudinal measures to instructors, but we may also find that some teachers differ in the degree to which they will accept imposed objectives in preference to those they might choose themselves.

There are also very practical problems associated with these tests, one of which is securing cooperation on the part of the public schools. We have encountered a fair amount of difficulty in securing participation by neighboring school districts. Even though it is generally conceded that research on this topic could be of considerable value to them, their policies often preclude such investigations. Frankly, many districts may be reluctant to assist in the development of teacher proficiency tests based on pupil achievement; some administrators may fear intrusion on their teacher-evaluation domain; and some teachers may feel genuinely threatened by the prospect of having their competence assessed in terms of pupil achievement. Until the performance tests have been demonstrated to be valid and helpful measures of at least this one aspect of teaching competence, we can anticipate some opposition to the tryout of our instruments.

Another problem is related to the actual validation test of these performance measures. Will the nonteachers' lack of familiarity with the pupils they are teaching prove to be the major deterrent to their successful accomplishment of the objectives? Must we set up a situation in which the nonteachers have an opportunity to work previously with the classes in order to allow them equal familiarity with the pupils? Or, on the other hand, should we set up this initial test so that we stack the deck as much as possible in favor of the experienced teachers? Since we wish to demonstrate that at a gross level these tests can discriminate between two extreme groups of instructors, perhaps we serve our purpose better if we do let the experienced teachers work with their own classes and the inexperienced teachers instruct unfamiliar pupils.

Related to this problem is the associated one that the nonteacher might attend more carefully to the given objectives because this would perhaps be the most obvious way of structuring his thinking regarding the instructional task. The experienced teacher would undoubtedly have a number of predilections regarding instructional pursuits, even though the particular subject matter unit might be unique in his school's curriculum. We may find that experienced teachers would actually suffer far more from distractions than the inexperienced teachers and would consequently tend to perform less effectively when performance is assessed exclusively by their ability to accomplish such prespecified instructional goals.

The most polished of our performance tests thus far developed is on the topic of carburetion in the field of auto mechanics. After three experimental versions, we now have a 27-page set of resource materials, including 29 specific instructional objectives and a large collection of possible learning activities, which is given to prospective participants in the study. We also have a 99-item post-test and a 20-item pre-test based on the 29 objectives, as well as a 17-item student questionnaire and a 16-item instructor questionnaire. All of these materials have been surveyed numerous times by vocational education consultants, usually junior college and high school auto mechanics instructors.

After extensive arrangements during the summer and fall of 1966, we tried out our carburetion performance test in a modest field test in the San Diego City Schools. All of the secondary school auto mechanics instructors of the San Diego schools were invited to participate in the project, and with only a few exceptions, all agreed to teach a 10-hour unit of instruction based on our performance test materials. Three of the instructors were selected for this field trial, and in addition, we secured the cooperation of several noncredentialed auto mechanics from a nearby U.S. Naval base who also agreed to participate in the project by using our materials to teach a class of high school youngsters. Both the regular credentialed teachers and the noncredentialed tradesmen were given a small honorarium for their participation in the project.

Three schools were involved in the study. It was originally hoped that both the experienced and nonexperienced teachers could be randomly assigned a class from the school's auto mechanics classes, thereby reducing the problem of preselection of a "good" class by the regular teachers. This was generally possible, although certain adjustments had to be made for the noncredentialed teachers that frequently resulted in their teaching an early morning or late afternoon class. The regular teachers were randomly assigned one of the remaining classes. Both groups of subjects, that is, three teachers and three nonteachers, were given the instructional materials at least ten days in advance of instruction and were told to teach the specified objectives, using any instructional procedures they wished, but that pre-tests and post-tests based on the explicit objectives cited in the materials would be administered by members of the research project staff. All subjects were encouraged to promote their students' attainment of the objectives. Pre-tests, post-tests, student questionnaires, and instructor questionnaires were administered by members of the research project staff.

Our hypothesis was that the experienced teachers would significantly outperform their noncredentialed counterparts. This very gross assessment of the validity of the performance test was considered to be a necessary first step in a systematic evaluation of the worth of the approach in assessing teacher competence.

From the pre-test and post-test means of the six subjects presented in Table 1, it can be seen that in all instances the experienced teachers performed better than their inexperienced counterparts. Although comparable scores were attained on the pre-test by pupils of the two groups, scores on the post-test all favored the experienced teachers. (This difference, using unit sampling by classrooms with N = 6, is significant according to a Mann-Whitney U test beyond the .05 level, one-tailed.)

Of the numerous variables under consideration as potential covariates that might be used for purposes of statistical control, the most eligible contenders on this occasion were (1) overall high school grade-point average, which evidenced a .55 correlation with post-test scores, and

(2) pupil questionnaire responses designed to reflect interest in the general field of auto mechanics, or more specifically, on the topic of carburetion (correlations between post-test scores and the latter type of questionnaire responses ranging near .50). As in previous field trials, the pre-test score appears to be of little predictive utility, the r between pre-test and post-test scores being $-.06$.

The results, then, of this extremely small-scale field trial with the carburetion performance test are rather encouraging. Although there are still a number of questions to be resolved, such as the difficulty of the post-test that only permits mean performance of well under 50 percent of its 99 items, the possibility of exercising some statistical control—by analysis of covariance, for example—seems more hopeful through the use of variables related to post-test performance with correlation coefficients of approximately .50, and between each other in roughly the same magnitude. For instance, the two possible covariates mentioned earlier, overall high school grade-point average and expressed interest in the topic, were correlated with each other at .54.

Several new considerations have emerged as a consequence of developmental work to date. For one thing, at the earliest conception regarding the use of these performance tests as measures of teaching competence, it was implicitly assumed that we could indeed develop a sufficiently sensitive index of a particular teacher's ability so that this measure might be used as a rating of *individual* instructors. The possibility, for example, of using results of one or more performance tests in merit-rating schemes did appear conceivable. Granted that problems of variability within different teachers' classes existed, it was thought that

TABLE 1

Carburetion Performance Test Field Trial:
Pre-test and Post-test Results

		Pre-test		Post-test	
	n	$\overline{X}$	s	$\overline{X}$	s
Teacher 1	25	9.2	3.0	37.8	18.4
Teacher 2	28	8.1	3.6	39.6	17.0
Teacher 3	26	9.6	2.7	42.0	16.3
Tradesman 1	20	8.3	3.3	33.9	19.9
Tradesman 2	26	8.1	4.3	29.3	18.9
Tradesman 3	26	9.8	2.8	37.3	17.8

this might be controlled, or at least adequately compensated for, through sensitive weighting procedures or simplified forms of statistical adjustment. It now seems that, in light of the grossness of the measurement device to be employed, we shall be very pleased if the performance tests are suitable for use only with *groups*. In other words, it will be a sufficient advance to develop a reliable group criterion measure that could be used in many educational situations; for example, to assess the efficacy of preservice or inservice teacher education programs.

Finally, the research to date has been designed to test the very simple hypothesis that experienced teachers will perform significantly better on these performance tests than inexperienced teachers. One wonders whether such a validity assessment is really necessary. Why should we not operationally define the teacher's ability to accomplish instructional objectives as the principal indicator of the teacher's effectiveness? It is obvious that there are other bases on which to judge whether a teacher is effective, but when these other indicators are compared with the teacher's ability to promote identifiable student growth, they seem far less defensible.

References

1. McNeil, John D., "Antidote to a School Scandal." *Educational Forum* 31 (November 1966), pp. 69–77.
2. Popham, W. James, and Eva L. Baker, "A Performance Test of Teacher Effectiveness." "Of Special Significance." *The Journal of Teacher Education* 17 (Summer 1966), pp. 250–51.

15

Performance Tests of Teaching Proficiency: Rationale, Development, and Validation

One of the most elusive targets in the history of educational research is a valid index of teacher effectiveness. Since the turn of the century literally hundreds of investigations have probed the question of teacher competence assessment and most of them have produced little, if any, significant progress.

In the last few years, however, evolving conceptions of the nature of instruction seem to offer promise to teacher effectiveness researchers. In most of the early investigations in which measures of teacher competence were sought, there was an almost exclusive focus on the instructional means employed by teachers. Researcher after researcher attempted to identify "good teaching procedures" for, should such procedures be discovered, they would obviously have implications for teacher education as well as for the evaluation of teachers on the job. Only recently have many educators come to accept the proposition that there are diverse instructional means which can be used to bring about a single instructional end. Teacher effectiveness research based on this assumption will tend to focus on the results achieved by instructors, not merely the means they employ.

When Morsh and Wilder (1954) in their definitive review of teacher effectiveness research during the first fifty years of this century indicated that no single teaching act had been discovered which was invariably associated with learner achievement, teacher competence researchers should have been more attentive. We should have first focused our efforts on identifying teachers who could produce superior growth in learners, leaving aside for the moment the question of how such improvements were brought about. If one can identify satisfactory measures of pupil attainment, then the next step is to identify the complicated procedures by which such achievements are attained. It is important to emphasize the complexity of this task, for the undoubted reason that

Reprinted by permission from *American Educational Research Journal*, Vol. 8, No. 1, January, 1971, p. 105.

reviewers such as Morsh and Wilder find few descriptions of "good teaching procedures" is that effective instruction represents a series of subtle interactions among a given teacher, his particular students, the instructional goals he is attempting to achieve, and the instructional environment.

Of course, there have been researchers who have employed the criterion of learner growth as an index of a teacher's proficiency. Such efforts would seem to represent proper attention to instructional ends rather than means. Most of these investigations relied upon the use of standardized achievement tests which, while comprehensive, rarely took into consideration the particular instructor's expectations regarding the outcomes to be measured. Further, the standardized measures employed were typically based on norm-referenced rather than criterion-referenced approaches to test construction (Glaser, 1963) and, as a consequence, were often inappropriate to measure group progress toward specified instructional goals.

Since the early 1960's we have witnessed a marked increase in research employing systematic classroom observation techniques. These efforts, perhaps best typified by the use of Flanders' Interaction Analysis procedures, have too frequently attended to classroom process variables without consideration of resulting modifications in learner behavior. Only recently (Campbell and Barnes, 1969) have a number of these investigations undertaken to report relationships between observation indices and learning outcome variables.

Because of the methodological difficulties encountered to date by teacher effectiveness researchers, a heretofore untried procedure for assessing teaching competence was conceived at the University of California, Los Angeles during 1964 involving the use of performance tests of teaching proficiency. Support was secured from the U.S. Office of Education for a four-year investigation designed to develop and subsequently test the validity of performance tests in the fields of social science, electronics, and auto mechanics.

Rationale

In brief, the general approach used in the performance tests of teaching proficiency calls for the development of a set of explicitly stated instructional objectives to cover a specified instructional period, in this case approximately ten hours. Coupled with such objectives are examinations based exclusively on the objectives. In addition, a collection of possible instructional activities and references is provided in a form comparable to the resource units found in so many curriculum libraries.

The procedure for using such performance tests requires that an instructor be given the objectives and resource materials well in advance of instruction. He is told to devise a sequence of instruction suitable for accomplishing the objectives and then allowed to teach to the objectives using whatever instructional procedures he wishes. In other words, only the ends are specified, the pedagogical means are left to the instructor. A teacher would be obliged, therefore, to accomplish the prespecified objectives, but would have freedom to choose instructional procedures which, to him, seemed likely to achieve those goals.

It is difficult, of course, to validate the merits of such an approach to the assessment of teaching competence. One does not have readily available the already established criterion measures which can be used to calculate concurrent validity coefficients. A construct approach to validation, therefore, appeared to be more appropriate. It seemed, considering the nature of the performance tests, that these measures ought to be able *at least* to distinguish between credentialed, experienced teachers and those who were neither credentialed nor experienced. In other words, if one were to take a group of credentialed, experienced teachers and ask them to teach to the objectives, in contrast to asking a group of "people off the street" to teach to the same objectives, the experienced teachers ought to out-perform their inexperienced counterparts. In order to test this validation hypothesis, it was proposed that performance tests be developed in the three fields previously mentioned and that the ability of the tests to discriminate between experienced teachers and nonteachers be determined. Results of developmental work and field tests will be described in the remainder of this article. More detailed descriptions of the research are available elsewhere (Popham, 1967; Popham, 1968).

Development

The developmental phase of this project involved the selection of a topic, statement of objectives, assembly of resource materials, and construction of test items. Any topic chosen had to meet several requirements. First, it should take 10 hours or less to teach, hopefully permitting us to secure cooperation from public school personnel who might be willing to devote two weeks of normal class time to our field trials but would be loath to give longer periods to the research. Second, to reduce the likelihood of previous student exposure to the material, the topic should not be currently taught in the schools. Third, the topic should require no specified set of student entry behaviors dependent upon previous instruction. Fourth, the topic should be able to be inserted logically at any point in the curriculum. A last requirement for the topic was that it be so acceptable to teachers that they would feel it important enough to employ.

Developmental work on the three performance tests, two in vocational education and one in the social sciences, occurred in the following pattern. First, topics meeting the above criteria which might be covered in two or three weeks were selected. These were then submitted to several subject matter specialists who served as consultants during the project. From these tentative topics, three were selected and instructional objectives were prepared which were also screened by consultants. A preliminary set of these objectives was agreed on, and test items based directly on the objectives were developed. In addition, possible learning activities and reference materials were assembled. In some instances, these learning activities were designed to be particularly pertinent to the given objectives. In other cases, the activities were planned to be appealingly exotic but not germane to the objectives. It was thought that less experienced instructors might be attracted to the irrelevant activities, but that the sophisticated teacher would tend to use the pertinent activities. These materials were revised several times prior to initial trials. Of course, it was possible that a teacher might choose to develop his own instructional activities without any reliance on the materials provided in the resource unit.

The early forms of the post-tests were given to several teachers for administration to classes of beginning and advanced students currently taking related vocational or social studies courses. Resulting data underwent item analysis procedures which led to the revision of many test items. When ready for the first field trial, all three performance tests consisted solely of objectives measurable by paper and pencil tests.

After extensive field trials with preliminary versions of the materials, one of the two vocational education tests was completely abandoned and a new topic selected. The other two tests, though seriously revised, were retained. When finally ready for the validation phase of the research, the following three performance tests were available:

Social Science Research Methods. This test, dealing with basic research techniques employed by social scientists, consisted of 13 specific instructional objectives, a 91-page resource unit, a 33-item pre-test, and a 68-item post-test.

Basic Power Supplies. This test in the field of electronics consisted of 23 specific instructional objectives, a 30-page resource unit, a 20-item pre-test, and a 46-item post-test.

Carburetion. This test in the field of auto mechanics consisted of 29 specific instructional objectives, a 27-page resource unit, a 20-item pre-test, and a 99-item post-test.

Validation

As indicated previously, we wished to test the hypothesis that the performance tests *at least* ought to be able to discriminate between experienced teachers and nonteachers with respect to their ability to accomplish prespecified instructional objectives. Thus, after developing the performance test materials, the next task was to locate a suitable number of teachers and nonteachers.

Subjects

The recruitment of subjects proved to be the most time-consuming operation of the entire research project. We solicited the cooperation of major metropolitan districts in which there would be a large number of teachers in the desired fields as well as numerous nonteachers who would have sufficient subject matter backgrounds to teach the units, but no prior teaching experience. In the case of the auto mechanics performance test we anticipated using garage mechanics from service stations, auto agency service departments, etc. For the electronics performance test we hoped to recruit individuals such as television repairmen and workers in the electronics industries. The nonteachers for the social science performance test might be drawn from housewives or college students with a social science background. Of all the large districts contacted throughout the state, only the San Diego City Schools agreed to participate in the project.

Beyond the location of school officials who would participate, there was also the problem of locating teacher volunteers as well as nonteachers who would agree to teach in the schools. Because of their extra effort involved in this project, an honorarium (for social science: $25; for electronics and auto mechanics: $50) was given to each participating teacher. A similar honorarium was given to each nonteacher participant.

Locating a sufficient number of nonteachers for the two vocational performance tests presented a considerable challenge. Personal contact with local industries failed to yield enough nonteachers who were both willing to participate in the project and could arrange their schedules in order to teach in the schools. We finally relied on saturation newspaper advertising in order to attract the attention of nonteachers. After several months of proselytizing, a sufficient number of teachers and nonteachers were located so that we had 28 pairs (teacher and nonteacher) for the auto mechanics field test and 16 pairs for the electronics field test.

There was far less difficulty encountered in locating nonteachers for the social science performance test field trials. The performance of 13 experienced teachers was contrasted with 13 San Diego State College students who had completed at least two years of college with a major or minor in social science.

All of the 13 social science teachers possessed a California teaching credential and a minimum of four years' teaching experience, several of them having taught for more than ten years. All of the 28 auto mechanics teachers and the 16 electronics teachers possessed a California teaching credential and had taught for at least two years, with a mean of five years of teaching experience for both types of vocational education teachers. None of the nonteachers in any of the three comparison groups possessed formal teaching experience or had completed previous teacher education coursework.

Procedure

All three performance tests were subjected to validation contrasts in ongoing school situations involving 2,326 public school students. There were slight differences between the procedures employed for the two vocational education tests and the social science test. Because of the necessity of controlling the potential influence of school effects in the data analysis, we located a nonteacher "match" for every teacher who agreed to participate in the project. For the two vocational education tests, teachers were selected who had at least two sections of a class in which the unit could be taught for approximately nine hours. For electronics, the following kinds of classes were usually involved: first and second year electronics and introductory electricity. For auto mechanics the following kinds of classes were generally involved: first and second year auto mechanics and power mechanics.

For the vocational education tests one of the classes was randomly designated as that which would be taught by the teacher. We were anxious to avoid the possibility that a teacher would select one of his best classes and, consciously or unconsciously, give a less able group to the nonteacher. In some instances, of course, the availability of a particular nonteacher dictated the selection of a certain class hour for him. In this instance, if more than one class remained which could be assigned to the regular teacher for the purposes of this project, the selection was made at random.

In general, the procedure for the electronics and auto mechanics tests involved giving the teacher and nonteacher sets of the instructional materials, that is, objectives and resource unit, approximately two weeks prior to the time when instruction was to commence. The nonteacher generally arrived at the school for the first time on the day instruction was to commence. He was introduced to the regular teacher by a member of the project research staff who then administered the pre-test to all students at the beginning of ten hours reserved for the project. The pre-test took approximately 15 to 20 minutes to complete. The regular teacher and nonteacher then, in their separate classes, taught for approximately nine hours. They attempted to achieve the objectives specified in the unit but, as indicated before, were free to use any instructional methods they wished. For legal purposes, while the nonteacher instructed, the regular teacher remained at the rear of the classroom but was directed not to interfere with the nonteacher's efforts or to collaborate in any way with the nonteacher in planning his instruction. At the conclusion of the nine hours of instruction, a member of the project staff administered the post-test to all students. A brief student questionnaire and instructor questionnaire were also filled out at the conclusion of the unit. In completing their questionnaires, the experienced teachers reported that they had refrained from involvement in the instructional activities of the non-teachers.

The tryout of the social science test, while essentially the same as for the two vocational education tests, was carried out somewhat differently. First, the instructional time allowed was only four hours. Second, the experienced teacher's regular class was randomly divided into two groups, one of which was taught in a separate room by the nonteacher. Again, for legal purposes a credentialed substitute unobtrusively remained at the rear of the nonteacher's classroom. At the close of the four-hour instructional period the post-test and questionnaire were administered to all students. Because of the random assignment to the two groups no pre-test was used.

Analysis

Because of the interaction among pupils in given classes, it was considered appropriate to treat the date in terms of classroom units rather than individual pupils. Accordingly, the first step in the analysis called for the calculation of classroom means for each of the variables involved in the investigation. These means constituted the data for subsequent analyses. The principal analysis concerned the prediction that teachers would significantly outperform nonteachers. The first analysis conducted to test this hypothesis was a correlated t test using the gross post-test score as the criterion. The correlated t model was employed because of the probable relationship associated with a teacher and nonteacher pair's being drawn from the same school. The correlation coefficients were .76, .60, and .23 for electronics, auto mechanics, and social science respectively. For the auto mechanics and electronics data an analysis of covariance was computed in which pre-test scores and students' expressed interest in the topic (on a five-point scale as reported in the questionnaire administered at the close of instruction) served as covariates. Due to the absence of pre-test data no analysis of covariance was computed for the social science data. Results of pupil-affective data on the post-instruction questionnaires were compared by analysis of variance. These analyses also involved classroom means rather than data for individual pupils.

Results

Results of the three contrasts involving t test comparisons of gross post-test scores are presented in Table 1 where it can be seen that differences of only a small magnitude existed between the teacher and nonteacher groups. Only in the case of the electronics data was the difference significant ($p < .05$, one tailed) on the basis of a correlated t test. A subsequent analysis of covariance in which post-test means were adjusted for initial pre-test differences (favoring the teacher group) failed to confirm this significant difference. The adjusted electronics means were almost identical, i.e., teachers: 23.9; nonteachers: 23.1. Analysis of covariance results for the auto mechanics and electronics contrasts are presented in Tables 2 and 3 respectively. Thus, in all three instances there were no significant differences between the ability of teachers and nonteachers to promote learner attainment of prespecified instructional objectives.

Analysis of variance tests of the difference between affective reactions of pupils, as reflected by responses to the student questionnaire, failed to reveal any significant differences between teacher classes

TABLE 1

Means, Standard Deviations, and Correlated t Test Results for Teacher and Nonteacher Classes

Test	Subjects	n	X°	s	t
Social Science	Experienced Teachers	13	33.4	2.2	.6
	College Students	13	32.3	3.0	
Auto Mechanics	Experienced Teachers	28	48.2	6.5	1.4
	Tradesmen	28	46.5	6.8	
Electronics	Experienced Teachers	16	24.3	4.5	2.0
	Tradesmen	16	22.7	3.8	

°Points possible: Social Science, 50; Auto Mechanics, 99; Electronics, 46.

TABLE 2

Analysis of Covariance of Auto Mechanics Classes
(Teachers Versus Nonteachers) Post-test Performance,
Using Pre-test Scores and Pupils' Expressed Interest
In Auto Mechanics as Covariates

Source	df	SS	MS	F
Between	1	22.7	22.7	.84
Within	52	1405.6	27.0	
Total	53	1428.3		

	Control Variables		Criterion Variable	
Group	Pre-test X	Interest X	Unadjusted Post-test X	Adjusted Post-test X
Teachers	9.8	3.6	48.2	48.0
Nonteachers	9.7	3.6	46.5	46.7

TABLE 3

Analysis of Covariance of Electronics Classes
(Teachers Versus Nonteachers) Post-test
Performance, Using Pre-test Scores and Pupils'
Expressed Interest in Electronics as Covariates

Source	df	SS	MS	F
Between	1	5.3	5.3	.72
Within	28	205.9	7.3	
Total	29	211.2		

	Control Variables		Criterion Variable	
Group	Pre-test X	Interest X	Unadjusted Post-test X	Adjusted Post-test X
Teacher	6.9	3.6	24.3	23.9
Nonteachers	6.8	3.5	22.7	23.1

and nonteacher classes. Measures involved in these analyses included responses to such questions as: "After this unit how would you rate your interest in the specific topic of carburetion?"

Discussion

Results of all three validation replications failed to confirm the prediction that experienced teachers would promote significantly better achievements of given instructional objectives than would nonteachers. In dealing with such results, one must consider the possibility of measurement or methodological deficiencies in order to explain away the unsupported hypothesis. The measuring instruments, however, appeared to be quite satisfactory. They satisfied criterion-referenced validity standards, that is, the test items were judged by a number of experts to be congruent with the stated objectives. There was certainly sufficient test ceiling in all three instances, with post-test performance never reaching 70 percent correct.

Methodologically, because of the desire to conduct the investigation in ongoing school situations, the teachers had several clear advantages over their nonteacher counterparts. The teachers were familiar with the school setting, e.g., classroom facilities, resource materials, etc. They knew their students, having worked with them for a number of weeks prior to the time the field tests were conducted. Couple these rather specific advantages with those which are typically attributed to teaching experience (such as skill in attaining classroom discipline, ease of speaking before students, sensitivity to the learning capabilities of particular age groups, etc.) and one might expect the teachers to perform much better on this type of task. The question is "Why not?"

Although there are competing explanations, such as insufficient teaching time, the explanation that seems inescapably probable is the following: *Experienced teachers are not particularly skilled at bringing about prespecified behavior changes in learners.* When it comes to a task such as that presented by the performance test in which they must promote learner attainment of specific instructional objectives, perhaps most experiencd teachers are no better qualified than a person who has never taught. To realize why this might be so, one needs only to speculate on the typical intentions of most public school teachers. They wish to cover the content of the course, to maintain classroom order, to expose the student to knowledge, and so on. Rarely does one find a teacher who, prior to teaching, establishes clearly stated instructional objectives in terms of learner behavior and then sets out to achieve those objectives.

Only recently, in fact, do we find many teachers who are even familiar with the manner in which instructional objectives are stated in measurable form.

Lest this sound like an unchecked assault on the teaching profession, it should be pointed out that there is little reason to expect that teachers should be skilled goal achievers. Certainly they have not been trained to be; teacher education institutions rarely foster this sort of competence. Nor is there any premium placed on such instructional skill after the teacher concludes preservice training. The general public, most school systems, and professional teachers' groups rarely attach special importance to the teacher's attainment of clearly stated instructional objectives.

To the extent that the foregoing analysis is accurate, the attempt to validate the performance test of teaching proficiency by contrasting the accomplishments of teachers and nonteachers was probably ill-conceived. It may have been wishful thinking to believe that experienced teachers would perform better. But the fact that this validation scheme was injudiciously selected does not mean that the performance-test approach is unworkable, nor that such tests cannot be validated.

This validation effort was an attempt to supply construct-validity evidence. Another more reasonable construct-validation approach could be based on a contrast between (a) instructors who had manifested measurable skill in promoting learner attainment of prespecified objectives and (b) instructors who had not manifested such skill. The initial group of instructors could be trained on comparable teaching tasks until they could show that when presented with instructional objectives specified in terms of learner behavior, they could accomplish such objectives. Then both the skilled and unskilled group could be given other performance tests such as those described in this report. The prediction would be, of course, that the skilled instructors display their generalized teaching proficiency by outperforming the unskilled instructors. In a similar vein, two investigators (Connor, 1969; Justiz, 1969) recently reported high positive correlations between teachers' achievements on two different short-term performance tests comparable to those described here. Such results are, of course, encouraging.

An additional caveat should also be mentioned. At the earliest conception regarding the use of these performance tests as measures of teaching competence, it was assumed that we could develop a sufficiently sensitive index of a particular teacher's ability to accomplish instructional objectives so that this measure might be used in evaluating individual instructors. The idea, for example, of using results of one or more performance tests in teacher merit rating schemes appeared possible. Granted that problems of variability among different teachers' classes existed, it was thought that this might be adequately compensated for through sensitive weighting procedures or other forms of statistical adjustment. It now appears, in light of the grossness of the measurement devices likely to be available in the near future, that we shall be pleased even if the performance tests are suitable for use only with groups. In other words, it will be a sufficient advance to develop a reliable group criterion measure which could be used in myriad educational situations such as to assess the efficiency of teacher education programs.

The principal conclusion of this project was that in three separate instances teachers were not able to perform better than nonteachers in their ability to promote learner attainment of prespecified instructional objectives. Obviously, generalizations beyond the types of teachers and nonteachers involved in the investigation, as well as the teaching task and pupils, should be undertaken cautiously. The explanation offered for these results was based on the teacher's lack of skill in achieving preset behavioral changes in learners.

References

CAMPBELL, JAMES R., and CYRUS W. BARNES, "Interaction Analysis—A Breakthrough?" *Phi Delta Kappan* 50 (1969), pp. 587–90.

CONNOR, AIKEN, *Final Report: Cross-Validating Two Performance Tests of Instructional Proficiency.* (Office of Education Project No. 8-1-174, Grant No. OEG 9-9-140174-0011(057), University of California, Los Angeles, December, 1969.)

GLASER, R., "Instructional Technology and the Measurement of Learning Outcomes: Some Questions." *American Psychologist* 18 (1963), pp. 519–21.

JUSTIZ, T.B., "A Method for Identifying the Effective Teacher." (Doctoral dissertation, University of California, Los Angeles. Ann Arbor, Mich.: University Microfilms, No. 29-3022-A, 1969.)

MORSH, JOSEPH, and ELEANOR WILDER, "Identifying the Effective Instructor: A Review of the Quantitative Studies, 1900–1952." (*Research Bulletin AFPTRC-T-54-44.* San Antonio, Texas: Lackland Air Force Base, 1954.)

POPHAM, W. JAMES, *Final Report: Development of a Performance Test of Teaching Proficiency.* (Office of Education Project No. 5-0566-2-12-1, Contract No. OE-6-10-254, University of California, Los Angeles, August, 1967.) (ERIC No. ED 013242.)

———, *Final Report: Performance Tests of Instructor Competence for Trade and Technical Education.* (Office of Education Project No. 5-004, Contract No. OE-5-85-051, University of California, Los Angeles, June, 1968.) (ERIC No. ED 027418.)

16

Found: A Practical Procedure To Appraise Teacher Achievement in the Classroom

Talk is cheap. While everyone's talking about the merits of educational accountability, few mention the fact that practical procedures for making accountability work have not been devised.

Tangible suggestions for implementing accountability systems have been made, however. One of the most interesting concerns use of the teaching performance test, a specific measurement tactic that can be employed in various accountability approaches.

Since the turn of the century, how to measure a teacher's instructional skill has perplexed a stream of educational researchers and evaluators. The most widely used measures—ratings, classroom observations, and pupil performance on standardized tests—all have proved dismally inadequate. They too often have been process-focused. They have tried to isolate "good teaching techniques" even though subsequent research strongly suggests that few, if any, pedagogical ploys invariably will work in all the instructional settings teachers encounter. If not process-focused, these measurement techniques often have failed to take into account the fact that different teachers pursue markedly different goals.

To eliminate some of these difficulties, a previously untried assessment technique, the teaching performance test, has been tested experimentally since 1965. While considerable research remains to be conducted on various aspects of teaching performance tests, results of their use in field trials suggest that they warrant further utilization.

A teaching performance test provides an estimate of a teacher's ability to produce a prespecified behavior change in a group of appropriate learners. Here's how it functions:

1. A teacher is given an explicit instructional objective along with a sample measurement item showing how the objective's achievement will be measured. He also receives background information on the objective.

Reprinted from the May, 1972, issue of *Nation's Schools*, Vol. 89, No. 5, p. 59. Copyright © 1972 by McGraw-Hill, Inc.

2. The teacher gets time to read the background information (if necessary) and to plan a lesson designed to achieve the objective.

3. The teacher instructs a group of pupils—as few as a half dozen or as many as a whole class—for a specified period of time.

4. The pupils are measured with a post-test based on the objective but unseen previously by the teacher. Pupil attitudes toward the instruction also are measured. These measures of pupil cognitive and affective results serve as an index of the teacher's effectiveness.

In general, the subject matter employed for each performance test is novel, thereby reducing the likelihood of the learner's previous familiarity with the topic. Because the same instructional objective is employed for all teachers completing a given performance test, legitimate comparisons can be made among different teachers' skill in accomplishing the preset objectives. This, of course, is the new measurement angle. By holding the instructional task constant, it is possible to contrast the ability of different teachers to get their pupils to master the task and demonstrate positive affect toward the instruction.

The trick, clearly, is to control other relevant conditions so that all teachers have the same opportunity to display whatever instructional skill they possess. This means randomly assigning learners to teachers and, if necessary, statistically adjusting for remaining inequities in disparate learners' entry behavior.

Right now teaching performance tests can play two valuable and practical roles in educational accountability systems. They can be used for *instructional improvement*—to help teachers get better at promoting beneficial changes in learners. And they can be employed for *skill assessment*—to discover which teachers are particularly good or particularly bad at this type of instructional task.

In the case of *personal* educational accountability, in which the teacher initiates any review of the results of his instruction, a teacher might use a performance test chiefly for instructional improvement. Either by himself or with invited colleagues, a teacher might work with different groups of children for short periods after school in successive efforts to improve his skill on a particular performance test or on a certain class of performance tests. Lessons that failed to achieve the objective or that promoted negative learner affect would be revised.

For *professional* accountability systems, in which a group of the teacher's colleagues initiates a review of his instruction, teaching performance tests can be employed for both instructional improvement and skill assessment. Groups of teachers, for example, might wish to foster the use of performance tests to help their colleagues get better at accomplishing instructional objectives. Teachers might be required by their colleagues to participate in a series of performance test clinics that featured post-lesson clinical analyses of the teachers' instructional decisions.

More important, perhaps, is the possibility that teacher organizations will seize upon the use of teaching performance tests as a skill assessment device to accomplish what they have always sought—control over entry into the profession. Consistent with a general thrust for professional responsibility, teacher organizations might set up procedures obliging aspiring teachers to display, along with other abilities, at least a minimum level of skill on teaching performance tests.

Finally, for *public* accountability systems, in which evidence regarding the quality of learner attainments is demanded by the public, the skill assessment use of performance tests may have merit. In an effort to make school systems answer for results, it is certainly plausible that the public might demand that teachers display at least minimal proficiency on performance tests.

The skill assessment approach also might help administrators select the most competent teachers applying for jobs. Administrators could set up a series of teaching performance tests, requiring three or four hours' time, to be completed by all applicants. This type of screening examination would be similar to the procedure whereby applicants for a given graduate school must complete, at their personal expense, the Graduate Record Examination. And since enrichment topics could be used for the performance test subject matter, any pupils from the district who participated in this screening process would be gaining new and useful knowledge.

As these illustrations have shown, the reason that the teaching performance test strategy should be particularly useful to proponents of educational accountability systems is its complete congruence with the central assumption of all accountability systems—a focus on the outcomes of instruction. To be sure, teaching performance tests assess only one competency of a teacher—his ability to achieve prespecified objectives. While that is only one criterion that should be used in evaluating a teacher, *it is a critical criterion.* Insofar as one believes the mission of teachers is to change children for the better, then any indicator of a teacher's skill in doing so should be given careful consideration.

Some will say, "But this isn't what teaching is really like. Teaching for a full day with 35 kids in a classroom is vastly different from teaching eight randomly assigned learners for a 30-minute lesson." Of course there are differences. But is there any reason to believe that a teacher who has performed miserably on several short-term performance tests will suddenly blossom in a regular teaching situation? Hardly.